C000044367

The Kiss of
The Father

Restoring a personal relationship
with the Holy Spirit

JULIAN ADAMS

RIVER
PUBLISHING

River Publishing & Media Ltd
Barham Court
Teston
Maidstone
Kent
ME18 5BZ
United Kingdom

info@river-publishing.co.uk

Copyright © Julian Adams 2015

All rights reserved. No part of this publication may be reproduced, stored in a retrieval system, or transmitted in any form or by any means, electronic, mechanical, photocopying or otherwise, without the prior written consent of the publisher. Short extracts may be used for review purposes.

Unless otherwise indicated, all Scripture quotations are taken from Holy Bible, New International Version®, NIV® Copyright © 1973, 1978, 1984, 2011 by Biblica, Inc.® Used by permission. All rights reserved worldwide.

ISBN 978-1-908393-48-7
Printed in the United Kingdom

Contents

What Others Are Saying About This Book

"I love Julian's honesty and down to earth approach. I know Julian and count him as my friend. He has written a book that is marked by truth, insight and practical illustrations that can only come from genuine encounter and trust in God. I believe it will help to release many who desire to move into the 'more' of God, and who yearn to walk in the power and fellowship of the Holy Spirit."
Mark Marx, Founder of Healing on the Streets and author of Stepping into the Impossible
www.healingonthestreets.com

"We owe a debt of gratitude to the prophetic and timely words of Julian Adams, whose new book invites us to be enriched, empowered and energised by the presence of the Holy Spirit in our lives. We have been called into the fellowship of the Son of God. The same participation of union between the Father and the Son is now ours by virtue of His finished work. That fellowship is impossible apart from the Holy Spirit, the third Person of the Godhead.

If you are hungry for the Father's kiss, then take time to partake of the rich insights Julian offers you in this powerful treatise on the work of the Holy Spirit in your life!"
Dr. Mark Chironna, Church On The Living Edge
Mark Chironna Ministries
Orlando, Florida

"Julian Adams beautifully invites us in this book to *know* Holy Spirit; not just know about Him, but to truly KNOW HIM. You will be filled with a hunger to grow in your relationship with God as you read and you will receive keys on how to posture yourself to receive the 'Kiss of God'."

Patricia King, Founder of XP Ministries
XPministries.com

"The mention of the presence of the Hoy Spirit often brings a look of apprehension. Julian has written a book which lets us push those fears aside and embrace the Holy Spirit with all He has for us and the Church of Jesus Christ. Julian brings to our attention the urgency to understand the need for both the presence and Person of the Holy Spirit. This is not something new, for Julian it has been his lifelong desire and has run through all he has done. From the days of being a toddler at prayer meetings, he was always around wanting to be part of what the Spirit of God was doing. As his dad, I was privileged to be a part of what the Holy Spirit was doing in Julian's life. The Holy Spirit's presence is as important to him now as it was then, and very much part of his ministry. *The Kiss of the Father* will create a desire for the Holy Spirit to be preeminent both in the church and our personal relationship with Him. Thank you, Julian, for bringing our attention back to the ministry of the Holy Spirit.

Chris Adams, Pastor of Father's House,
Simon's Town, South Africa

"Julian Adams, in a powerful and clear prophetic voice, is calling the Church to a deeper intimacy and friendship with

the Person of the Holy Spirit – an utterly childlike trust in Him. I love the fact that the Holy Spirit admonished him by telling him: 'Son, I want you to *grow up and become a child*'! This book is a must read for all who are seeking a fresh encounter with God."
Rev Lazarus Yeghnazar, President, 222 Ministries International

"I love Julian Adams. Whenever I have ministered with him I have been richly blessed by his revelation, impressed by his character, and inspired by the profound way he hears from the Lord. As I have gotten to spend time with him over the years, I have seen that this flows from a deep passion for Jesus, a love of the Father, and a friendship with Holy Spirit. As you read this book you will hear his heart, be touched by his testimony and stirred by his insights. Holy Spirit is much more than a wind, or a faceless force, or a pull of conviction.

Holy Spirit is the very Person of God, the great gift of our Father made possible through the incredible sacrifice of Jesus. He longs to draw each of us into the adventure of discovery, intimacy and empowerment that is getting to know and connect with Him in a much deeper way than simple theological understanding. Allow Julian to introduce you to His dear friend, Holy Spirit, and discover that He wants to be your dear friend, too."
Robert Hotchkin, XP Ministries
XPmedia.com/channel/rhotchkin

"We are privileged to have known Julian for many years, recognising his prophetic and apostolic anointing, but know him first and foremost as a very dear friend. His ministry has

shaped our lives. What stands out is that the man and the message are one. Julian has a sound knowledge of the subject matter and models an authentic, deep friendship with the Holy Spirit. A warning: reading this book might leave you with a slightly uncomfortable sense of longing for more of God's presence and power in your life. It did that for us!"
Arno and Margarete Schubert, Face à Face Church,
Rennes, France

"We have come to know, love and value Julian firstly as a person, but also value and appreciate his prophetic ministry. He has spoken amongst the family of churches in Relational Mission in recent years and his input has been rooted in love for God and His Word and has brought encouragement, strengthening and comfort to the churches. Such features are some of the hallmarks of genuine prophetic ministry."
Mike Betts, Apostolic Leader, Relational Mission

"I have never been more aware of the urgent need of the Church to reach and disciple 'the multitudes in the valley of decision' than I am now. Whether in the midst of the urban cry of our cities or the sprawling masses of India, we are to continue the mission and ministry of Jesus as He did: BY THE POWER AND LOVE OF THE SPIRIT, in word and deed! This book comes at this urgent time, when so many believers are being seduced by a pragmatic yet powerless form of Christianity that will serve to entertain the waiting nations, but never transform them by the power of the gospel. I believe this book will help unlock the Church into her original design: powerfully loved by the Father and powerfully changing the world in which we live. Not only do I joyfully endorse this well written, authentic, engaging and provoking book, I also endorse my friend Julian Adams who lives, himself, under the kiss of the Father."

Ryan Matthews, Senior Leader, Glenridge Church
Durban, South Africa

Dedication

For Fay MacBeath,
a lover of the Holy Spirit

Acknowledgements

To the Kings Arms community. Thanks for pioneering a church that is sensitive to the Holy Spirit.

Simon and Caroline Holley, you guys have loved me to a place of wholeness and freedom. I stand amazed that God would add you to my life.

Benny Hinn, I watched you as a young boy and instantly fell in love with your relationship with the Holy Spirit. Thank you for introducing me to Him.

Terry Virgo, your message of a Spirit-filled Church should be preached all over the world. It has ruined me for predictable, cookie-cut meetings.

Fay MacBeath, your prophecy over me has guided me and overtaken me with incredible breakthroughs and favour. You saw me preaching in Europe long before anyone else did. You have entered into your reward and I trust that your heavenly bank account is still gaining interest because of my life, which you impacted.

To many friends who have loved me and partnered with me. Thanks you for being there for me!

My Mum and Dad, you have lived a life of integrity and faithfulness to God in the midst of very trying situations and have been the primary revelation of who Holy Spirit is to me. Thank you.

Katia Adams, Wow! What a gift God has given to me in you. Your constant love for the Holy Spirit and infectious smile make me the happiest man in the world. You have believed in me and pulled destiny from me in a unique way. This book is a result of your encouragement. I Love you so, so much.

Foreword by David Devenish

I am so pleased that Julian Adams has written this book about our personal relationship with the Holy Spirit. Even within the Charismatic Church, it is possible for believers to experience the power and gifts of the Holy Spirit without an appreciation of the intimate nature of a relationship with the Holy Spirit as a Person. Julian's book, *The Kiss of The Father*, has reminded me of my own early experiences and understanding of the Holy Spirit.

My first encounter with the Holy Spirit in this way came as a result of reading an account by the English preacher, Dr Martyn Lloyd-Jones, of Thomas Goodwin, one of the Puritan fathers of 300 years ago. Goodwin pictured a man walking along a road with his little boy, holding hands. The little boy knows that the man is his father and that his father loves him. Suddenly that father stops, picks up the boy, lifts him up into his arms and embraces him. Then he puts him down again. As Goodwin says, the boy is no more a son than he was before but what a difference in the enjoyment! This was Goodwin's account of the personal experience of the Holy Spirit and the Father's love which helped lead me to experience this for myself many years ago. Julian's book conveys a contemporary reminder of this ancient truth that many have enjoyed over the centuries. Sadly, however, some Christians fall short in their experience even though they have received it as a doctrine. My heartfelt prayer is that all who read this book will enter into a personal relationship with the Holy Spirit and, by the Holy Spirit, experience the love of the Father in a tangible way.

David Devinsh
Catylist Apostolic Leader
Author of Demolishing Strongholds

Foreword by Dr Pete Carter

I first met Julian in 2004 when I went to speak at his church in Cape Town, South Africa. My wife and I were visiting our daughter, Kerry, who was spending a year there working with another church. As part of that she received theological training and Julian was one of the speakers.

Kerry told us, "You must meet this young guy, Julian Adams, he is amazing." And so we met Julian one Sunday and this started a friendship. We found a young man with a great sense of humour and fun, and a very strong and accurate prophetic gift, alongside humility and wisdom. Indeed, a rare combination in such a young man.

Later that year he visited our church near London, UK, and spoke at a meeting and had an extraordinary impact upon us. He prophesied over individuals and the whole church in a way that encouraged, inspired and directed us. One of the prophesies given that day still directs and informs our priorities and actions as a church.

Over the years our friendship has grown and we have done endeavours together in extending the kingdom of God. I have witnessed an increase in anointing and depth of gifting over the years, along with the ability to convey biblical truth, and at all times I have been aware of Julian's friendship with Holy Spirit.

The Kiss of the Father is not a book of theory, it is a book based on the experience of, and the study of God, the Father, Son and Holy Spirit. Julian's personal relationship with God shines through as he explains theological truths backed up with practical experience. After all the word "theology" means "the knowledge of God" and without personal experience we will end up with a dry experience. I can assure you that being around Julian is certainly not that. Truths about the Father's heart and His promises to His children, Jesus the anointed one, and the Person of the Holy Spirit will lead the reader into a deeper journey of faith, travelling into the practical outworking of relating to Holy Spirit, the power of speaking in Tongues, uncontainable Joy, the importance of an eternal perspective, and how to receive more of God's full reality in our everyday lives.

This is a rich book which will enrich your life. At times, whilst reading it, I found myself pausing to contemplate an expansion of my understanding and then expressed my gratitude to God for His amazing love, power and wisdom. I commend this book to you, not just as a piece of literature, but as a journey of discovery with my good friend, Julian Adams.

Dr Pete Carter
Author of Unwrapping Lazarus
Senior Leader of "Eastgate"
(formerly North Kent Community Church)

Chapter 1

The Spirit Himself

"You place too much emphasis on the Holy Spirit."

This is what a pastor told me after a meeting where many people had encountered the Holy Spirit for the first time. Many were filled with His presence, numbers experienced great joy, and others were filled that evening. This assessment came from a well-meaning pastor who wanted his church's ministry focus to be on expository preaching from the Bible. I have a very strong commitment to biblical truth, but I felt compelled to reply, "I place emphasis on the Holy Spirit because He is God!"

Whilst many Christians have a theological understanding of the Holy Sprit as a person, revealed as God, I have come to believe that not so many experience Him in this way. Instead, He is perceived more as a "force" than a person. This sounds like a strong statement, and it is, because if we don't understand the personhood of the Holy Spirit, then it makes us similar to the Jehovah's Witnesses, who believe the Holy

Spirit is a force like the wind. Dare I say it, many evangelicals, regardless of what they believe, treat the Holy Spirit in this impersonal way. At best He is regarded as a "veiled expression of God". Many Christians don't seem to relate to Him in any way other than for empowerment for service.

In the words of R A Torrey, "If we think of the Holy Spirit as so many do as merely a power or influence, our constant thought will be 'how can I get more of the Holy Spirit?' But if we think of him in a biblical way as a divine person, our thought will rather be, 'How can the Holy Spirit have more of me?'"

Much has been taught in recent years about the distinction between the Word and the Spirit. As a reaction to what some have seen as excess in the Charismatic Church, there has come a renewed emphasis on the Word. Of course, it is right to emphasise the Word, it is God's truth, but in the process, our understanding of the role of the Spirit has been reduced. Some have settled for an unholy trinity of God the Father, God the Son and God the Holy Bible! The Holy Spirit, however, is not some unseen force – this would contradict all we know that is revealed about Him in the Bible. Bill Johnson makes this radical statement: "We sometimes value a book the early church did not have over a person (the Holy Spirit) they did have."

I am intentionally overstating this fact to prove a point: we seem to be trying to replicate early Church Christianity without the emphasis of the early Church – the work of the Spirit! Many Christians theology of the Holy Spirit recognises that He is coequal, coexistent with, and is indeed God. But theology is of no use to anyone unless it is lived out. The Bible is full of references to the person of the Holy Spirit. He seems to be the first and the last revelation of God in the Bible.

"In the beginning, God created the heavens and the earth. The earth was without form and void, and darkness was over the face of the deep. And the Spirit of God was hovering over the face of the waters." (Genesis 1:1-2).

At the very beginning, God's Spirit is revealed. He is creative, powerful and the life-giver to all mankind. He is the self-revealing, self-sustaining God and is God in every way that God is God! Then, He is the one who is preparing the Church for the imminent return of Jesus, encouraging us to cry, "Maranatha! Come Lord Jesus! He is known as the "Eschatos", the one who will bring the fullness of the Kingdom to the earth. He is the one in whom the Kingdom is found! (Romans 8:14-17)

Somehow, many Christians do not know what to do with the Holy Spirit. He is often relegated to being the "butler of heaven", simply carrying out what the rest of the Trinity wants. But whilst He is indeed the empowering presence of God in the life of the believer, I have come to know him as much more than that.

My experience

My journey with the Holy Spirit began at a young age. I grew up in a Pentecostal/Charismatic household. Life at home was always an adventure where church was concerned. My parents sought out meetings where God was moving in amazing ways. We would go there and wait on the Holy Spirit to manifest His presence. When He did break in, it was exhilarating. It was just like the biblical examples we read of people being filled with the Spirit. People began to speak in other tongues, people prophesied and many came under the "unction" of the Spirit's power. Signs and wonders would often be a hallmark of these meetings and many would go home happy in God.

I had a deep longing and yearning to experience God in this way from a young age. I was filled with the Spirit when I was just three years old, and from the age of four onwards began speaking in tongues. My experience of the Spirit set me apart with a desire to be in ministry. Even at the age of four I had the clear sense that God had called me to serve Him in a way that would require all my time.

I recognised the presence of the Holy Spirit in my life and would often talk to Him. I began to develop a real sense of intimacy with Him. This affected the way I lived as a young man. Even though I was by no means an angel, I was certainly aware of the leading of the Holy Spirit.

At the age of 9 I received a prophetic word from a lady who would later become a great influence on me called Janet Brann. She spoke of me being anointed by God in a special way and said that I would go into ministry one day. She said a number of other things that day which unlocked an even deeper desire in me to be in God's presence. Something happened in me that day – I began to be more aware of the voice of the Spirit. It was then that I began to prophesy. A little later a family friend, Fay MacBeath, prophesied over me that I would be a prophet to the nations. This was humbling and, at the same time, exciting that God could use me in this way.

It was shortly after I turned 14 that I first came across the book "Good Morning Holy Spirit" by Benny Hinn. I was struck by the following words: "What I want you to know is this: beyond salvation, beyond being baptized in water, beyond the infilling of the Spirit, the 'third person of the trinity' is waiting for you to meet Him personally. He yearns for a lifelong relationship. And that is what you are about to discover."

As I read the book I came alive to the reality of a deeper intimacy with the Holy Spirit than I had known. Yet, the Bible calls us to this kind of intimacy with Him. Paul's parting words to the church at Corinth are a commendation to intimacy with the Holy Spirit:

"The grace of the Lord Jesus Christ and the love of God and the fellowship of the Holy Spirit be with you all." (2 Corinthians 13:14)

The word "fellowship" here describes communion, partnership and intimacy. Elsewhere Paul points out that our daily lives depend on the leading of the Spirit . In fact, it is a mark of our sonship (Romans 8:14). A personal relationship with the Spirit is what we have been called to.

Holding Him at arm's length
Why is it then that many Christians don't enjoy the kind of intimate personal relationship with the Holy Spirit that the Bible indicates we should have?

I believe one reason is a fear of the supernatural. Some believers are scared, or at least very wary of, the supernatural because they don't want to be deceived and they worry about being drawn into "fleshly" spiritual manifestations – particularly certain physical responses to the Holy Spirit, such as shaking, laughing, falling over etc.

Intertwined with this is our fear of not being in control,

or of being exposed. Though they may not acknowledge it, many people have a deep down fear that if they relinquish control to the Holy Spirit, he will expose them and others will learn about their secret sins. But the Holy Spirit never does this, because He is God by nature and so loving, kind and protective.

I mentioned the second, major, reason at the beginning of this chapter. There exists in the Church a lack of understanding of the Holy Spirit's personhood, character and mission.

The Holy Spirit is a person – a true reflection of the Godhead; one of the trinity; the promise of the father. He is the joy in our sonship and the power in our mission. He is my best friend and I love Him. It is therefore surprising to me that most systematic theology texts are weak on the person of the Holy Spirit, in stark contrast to Pentecostal theology, which is rich in truth about the Holy Spirit.

However, many of my friends who would have called themselves cessationists, now see the theological importance and value of a clear teaching that embraces the gifts of the Holy Spirit as a functional part of every believer's life. My friend, Terry Virgo, who is one of my heroes, has done much to help others' understanding of life in the Spirit – and he has seen significant breakthroughs in previously non-Charismatic movements because of his high view of Scripture. Many from a traditionally conservative background are now open to the work of the Spirit. I am so grateful to Terry and, of course, God for this – it will make it easier for the next generation to articulate the work of the Spirit.

Why has the cessationist view persisted in the Church? I believe it has to do with the fact that evangelical theology owes much to St Augustine, the first of the Church fathers to propagate the theory that the Holy Spirit's gifts died with the last of the Apostles. But later, there are accounts of Augustine's ministry that include records of God performing miraculous healings through him.

Finally, many don't enjoy the relationship with the Holy Spirit that they ought to out of some sense of false humility. Historically, many have been (badly) taught that we are not to run after the gifts of the Spirit, but to run after Jesus. At first glance this sounds "spiritually sound" but actually it's not. Jesus sent the Spirit to be with us daily on Earth and He expects us to partner with the Spirit. Then, the Spirit always wants to give glory to Jesus, so why are we afraid that embracing Him will detract from Jesus?

Set free to be yourself

This book is given over to discovering more about the Holy Spirit. This process should be fun and an adventure of discovery. I could list all the scriptural attributes that prove the Holy Spirit is a co-equal with the Father and Son, to prove His place and person in the Trinity, but the evidence is there for you to discover and that's not what this book sets out to do. Knowledge about the Spirit is important, but friendship with Him is what I want to see released in you.

So let's journey together. I am hoping you will discover the incredible person the Holy Spirit is. Descriptions like wind, fire, water and various other biblical images are great, but when you understand that the Holy Spirit is a person, with all the characteristics we expect a person to have, our engagement with Him will be a lot more exciting. The Holy Spirit has an opinion on everything – after all He is the Spirit of truth. He wants to interact with us on a very deep level – to comfort and nurture us, to set us free and remind us of who we really are.

The Holy Spirit is so free and so powerful. He is the one who takes ordinary flesh and gives us an unfair advantage! I want to provoke you to get to know Him properly; to live a life led by the Spirit; to enjoy friendship, intimacy and communion with Him. I pray that this book helps you to achieve that.

"In him you also, when you heard the word of truth, the gospel of your salvation, and believed in him, were sealed with the promised Holy Spirit." (Ephesians 1:13)

Chapter 2

The Kiss of the Father

The performance trap

I grew up in church. My dad was a pastor. I once tried to work out how many church meetings I've attended in my life in total. I lost count, but I know I have a pretty high average. I was different to other kids my age growing up, because I really wanted to be at church all the time. I got upset when I couldn't go. In fact, I tried every trick in the book to convince my parents I needed to go to certain meetings. A close family friend who was an evangelist once wrote a song in my honour. It was called, "Preacher man, don't ever leave me at home." It's safe to say that I really loved church!

From the age of fifteen I began ministering alongside my dad in meetings. I have many memories of God's power breaking in and touching the lives of many hurting or sick people. These occasions are indelibly printed on my mind as very special events. Alongside this, I loved the Word of God and took great pride in studying the Bible.

I attended a Bible school run by our youth pastor, which aimed to equip young people with the basic truths of our faith. Unfortunately, I took pride in studying the Bible in order to prove a point. I had a strong desire to seek God, but I also became filled with the need to "defend" Him and His truth. This meant that I soon became intense and uncompromising (which I thought was very spiritual) in the expression of my faith. I rammed the gospel down people's throats at every opportunity and carried around some truly cringe worthy Christian paraphernalia. My school bag was emblazoned with "I [heart] JESUS" in big, bold print. Talk about cheesy!

Outwardly I looked every bit the uncompromising zealot. Inside though, was a different story. All the while I was blazing the trail for Jesus I was struggling to make sense of my own inadequacies and failures. I was a "great" Christian on the outside, but I couldn't keep up the façade and inside I began to crumble. I became judgmental and angry with anyone who appeared less spiritual than me – most notably at home with my family. I became pharisaical towards my siblings. Whenever they did something wrong, not behaving like pastor's kids should, I jumped on it because it made me feel better about myself. I had caught the serious disease of religion and it was beginning to affect me.

My passion for Jesus was replaced by an intensity that was merely a mask for the religious spirit. I found myself in the trap of performance – I had a purely works-based relationship with God. I took pride in my biblical knowledge and my regular quiet times. I began to gage my intimacy with Jesus by how well I was doing on my spiritual scorecard. Yet, in my heart of hearts, I knew I was as far from God as I could be! By the time all of this dawned on me I had graduated from Bible school and was working full time for a church.

I could see the cracks appearing, but the façade of hard work for Jesus simply increased. More meetings, more prayer times, and more fasting simply added to my spiritual pride, whilst doing nothing to reduce my sinful attitudes, thoughts and actions. In short, I had become a professional Pharisee. To everyone else I looked amazingly spiritual, but I knew that my passion for Jesus was waning and I was in trouble.

It's amazing how long one can continue as a professional Pharisee. A number of years went by and I was still working hard at being a "good Christian". I was really bad at it and still unhappy. Then I began to notice what was happening to my peers. Those I had thought unspiritual and worldly were suddenly being promoted into positions of leadership in the church, having seemingly spent a long time doing their own thing and ignoring God. Now, having surrendered to God, there were being led by His grace and were enjoying Him a lot more than I was! Remember the older brother in the parable of the prodigal son? The one who hears the sounds of celebration and asks, "What's going on?" I was that older brother; I couldn't recognise the sound of a good party because I'd been baptized in lemon juice!

I continued living in the bondage of performance for many years until one day when I heard Terry Virgo speaking in a high school in Cape Town. He was preaching from Titus 2:11:

"For the grace of God has appeared that offers salvation to all people."

As Terry expounded the truths of the glorious gospel of grace I heard the message as if for the first time. It was revolutionary. I suddenly began to understand that God's grace had made a way for me to live like a son instead of a slave (Galatians 4:7).

That night I experienced such freedom from sin and the need to perform in order to "earn" God's grace. All the way home I chatted to a friend of mine about what we'd heard. I was rejoicing that my performance as a Christian was not the basis for my acceptance and sonship. That night "grace" became for me more than a girl's name or something I said before I ate! It became the doorway by which I could enter God's presence and approach the Father with complete confidence. (If you've never come across Terry Virgo, please get hold of his book, God's Lavish Grace – it is a brilliant book containing teaching foundational to the Christian life).

The Father's pleasure

When Jesus was baptized in the river Jordan (Luke 3:21-22) something amazing happened. The heavens opened and the Holy Spirit descended and remained on Jesus. Then the voice of the Father said, "You are my Son, in you I am well pleased." The Father expressed His utter delight in His Son.

It's a very familiar passage, but here is the important point: up until this point, Jesus had performed no miracles or done any works which might have impressed anyone or earned the Father's affirmation. There had been no significant display of Jesus' abilities as the Son of God. Yet, the Father is pleased to shower Jesus with His favour. No performance on Jesus' part – just complete pleasure on the Father's part. Jesus is our role model and this truth applies to us too: we can do nothing to earn the Father's favour, He just accepts us and takes great pleasure in us as His children. We don't need to perform and we cannot earn it.

Another staggering truth is revealed in the context of these verses. John's gospel tells us that the way John the Baptist knew Jesus was the genuine Son of God was because the Holy Spirit rested and remained upon Him. Modern Christians can somewhat take for granted the miracle of the Holy Spirit dwelling within us, but with Jesus something completely radical was taking place.

The Old Testament understanding of an encounter with the Holy Spirit was that it was a temporary experience. He came and rested on people for a season – and then it was only priests, kings and prophets who experienced Him (apart from the odd donkey!) In other words, only a select few knew the joy of deep intimacy with the Holy Spirit. Remember David's prayer in Psalm 51:10-11:

"Create in me a clean heart, O God, and renew a right spirit within me. Cast me not away from your presence, and take not your Holy Spirit from me." (ESV)

The way in which John could recognise that Jesus was the son of God was through the outpouring of the Holy Spirit upon His life. Something altogether new was happening: the Holy Spirit had made His abode with Jesus. The earth had not known a man on whom the Holy Spirit not just rested on, but remained with. The beginning of Jesus' mission, then, was birthed in the person of the Holy Spirit. He lived His whole life submitted to the Holy Spirit. He was led by the Spirit. He performed His miracles by the Spirit's power. Jesus is the model of the Spirit filled life, with its foundation built on the complete love, acceptance and affirmation of the Father.

The Father's promise

People often view the Holy Spirit as "the one who helps us do stuff for God". In fact, the primary role of the Spirit is to witness with us that we are sons of God. He is what I call "the Family Spirit" – He is the one who marks us out as belonging to God's family, sons and daughters of the Father. He is like the seal or signet ring of the Father. He is known as the Spirit of adoption.

When Jesus was nearing the completion of His mission on earth, He told His disciples, "I will not leave you as orphans..." (John 14:18). He was about to go through the trial of the cross, then resurrection and ascension to heaven. He was going to the Father and was promising to pour out the Holy Spirit on His disciples. He continues to pour out His Spirit on all who put their trust in Him. The same authenticating mark of the Holy Spirit that identified Jesus as the Son of God is upon us, to mark us out as sons of God!

The Bible calls the Holy Spirit the promise of the Father. He comes to help us understand who we are and to help us know and experience the Father. He is the one who causes us to cry, Abba (Daddy!) The Holy Spirit brings both identity and affirmation. As Christians, our mission on the earth is not simply to do with the message we bring, it was inextricably wrapped up in our identity as sons. Jesus said to His disciples, "As the Father has sent me, I am sending you." This was not just a mission mandate, it was a statement of relationship: we are sons of a relational father and we cultivate our relationship with Him simply by being sons.

I find it fascinating that a great deal of our generation has been crippled by a lack of fathers. In South Africa, one of the ways that the apartheid government would keep the black majority subdued was to separate fathers from their families and send them to different locations to work. This strategy seems to have been used throughout history. Around us we see the devastating effects of a generation who have not enjoyed the privilege of having a father around. Many of the problems faced by contemporary South Africa have their roots in a lack of fatherhood – and I believe this is true of many other societies around the world.

Once, I was attending the Newday youth conference in the UK and my friend, Joel Virgo, was speaking from Ephesians 6 about how children should honour their parents. It was an incredibly moving message. The jam-packed 6,000-seater tent became all the more cramped as young people began to do what Joel encouraged them and responded to God's word. At that moment I felt the Lord drop a word of knowledge in my heart about adopted children not being able to receive love from their parents. God was saying that some were finding it hard to accept a fathering love and were even lashing out in anger towards their adoptive parents.

A young man approached me after the meeting, weeping because he had realised he was doing that very thing. I prayed with him to receive the Holy Spirit and to come under the "Spirit of Adoption". Unbeknown to me, his adoptive parents had come to the end of their tether with this young man. He had become violent and abusive, and had had to be moved out of home to live with a family in church, because the tension was so bad. He had been given counselling and his psychologist called his problem an "attachment disorder" – a common problem among adopted children who find it hard to connect and receive love from adoptive parents.

That night, however, after receiving prayer, he phoned his adoptive parents and asked for their forgiveness. God had begun the process of healing his hard heart. He described his heart as being like an impenetrable metal tank filled with a load of gunk and said that Jesus had come along and broken it open – all the putrid gunk inside had drained away.

In the same way, there are many "children" in the Church who are living with an "attachment disorder" concerning their heavenly Father. They may have accepted in theory the fact that they have been adopted into the family of God, but they are struggling to receive His love and acceptance. They are not yet secure enough in their identity to cry out "Daddy!" They need to experience greater intimacy with the Spirit of adoption.

After preaching on the Spirit of adoption one time, a gentleman who had been in ministry for many years came up to me and said, "This is the first time in years of ministry that I really understand that I am a son!" In the same meeting, a young guy who had grown up in one of the tough housing estates of inner city London came to me and said, "I've never known my father, but tonight I've met the Father!" Such revelation only comes from the Spirit!

The Father's kiss

I love the story of the prodigal son in Luke 15. A son leaves his home to live a life of sin and disregard for his father. He squanders his inheritance. Eventually, after living in a pig pen, he comes to his senses and decides it's a good idea to go home to his father's house. As he approaches home, one translation says that his father ran to him and "fell on him and kissed him". The boy didn't even get the chance to deliver his well rehearsed speech of repentance – the father simply embraced him, expressed joy over his return, then threw a huge party for him. He lavished the best he had on his son and extravagantly blessed him.

The bit I love is the father falling on the son and kissing him. It is a beautiful picture of how the Holy Spirit is given to us. The phrase "fell on" in Luke 15 is the same phrase used to describe the Holy Spirit falling on the believers in the book of Acts. The Holy Spirit is the "kiss of the Father". St Bernard of Clairvaux (1091-1135) expressed it like this:

"If, as is properly understood, the Father is he who kisses, the Son he who is kissed, then it cannot be wrong to see in the kiss the Holy Spirit, for he is the imperturbable peace of the Father and the Son, their unshakable bond, their undivided love, their indivisible unity." (St Bernard's commentary on his "Sermon 8" on Song of Songs)

Depending on the nature of your relationship with your father, you may find this an alien concept. For me, personally, it's not. In my culture, whenever my dad sees me he kisses me, because I'm his son. No other man gets to kiss me, just my dad. In fact, if someone else tried, I would find it very strange! My dad is the one who kisses me.

In the same way, the Holy Spirit poured out on us is the affection of the Father – a constant reminded of our sonship. He loves us with an everlasting love. His love is not soppy or weak, it is powerful and life changing. It is powerful enough to heal the sick and restore the broken hearted. It raised Jesus from the dead!

In the parable, the father says something staggering to his older son: "Son, you are always with me, and all that is mine is yours" (Luke 15:31)

Our access to the resources of heaven, our freedom to receive revelation, comes from a radical understanding that we are sons. We can enjoy all that is in our Father's house at any time. What marks someone out as a son is that they have free reign in their father's house. Yet, despite his status, the older brother was no better than a slave in his father's house, because he had a slave's mind set. He had an attachment disorder. He never took advantage of the fact that he could celebrate at any time he wanted. He didn't understand that he was called simply to be a son, before he worked for his father.

We receive the joy of sonship by receiving the Spirit of adoption. A spiritual "transaction" takes place when we receive the Holy Spirit. It is the Spirit who brings us into the unfolding revelation of our sonship and the Father's heart toward us.

Under the Old Covenant we were tutored by the Law, but now God has sent us the Holy Spirit, by which we cry out "Abba! Father!" (Galatians 4:1-7). He is the guarantee of our inheritance. It is by the Spirit that all Jesus accomplished on the cross becomes freely available to us. Life in the Spirit is the most exhilarating adventure of seeing God and hearing His voice!

Biblical commentator Ben Witherington says, "Sonship and the reception of the Spirit of God are not regarded as separate, but are instead inextricably linked: the Spirit comes with sonship ... it is in no way dependent on law- keeping!"

J. I. Packer says, "God adopts us out of His free love, not because our character and record shows us worthy to bear his name, but despite the fact that they show the opposite. We are not fit for a place in God's family; the idea of His loving and exalting us sinners as he loves and has exalted the Lord Jesus sound ludicrous and wild – yet that and nothing less than that, is what our adoption means." (Knowing God)

We are set apart by God for sonship. The Holy Spirit works in us to release in us the likeness of the Father and to set us free to be all He wants us to be.

No more pressure

All of this means that the pressure to perform in order to be "accepted" is completely redundant. However, we have such a propensity to try and earn God's favour that we need to remain vigilant. We so easily slip back into performance. The only way to counteract this is to remain immersed in God's presence, continually being filled with His Spirit – because the Holy Spirit reminds us of our adoption and total acceptance.

Being involved in the prophetic ministry, people often try to put you on a pedestal, as if you are the very oracle of God. Often, at the end of a meeting, people queue up, pressing in to have me pray for them. I find people's desperation to hear from God both moving and frustrating. Moving because I know people genuinely want to hear from Him; frustrating because they can hear from their Heavenly Papa any time they want because of the Holy Spirit.

In such situations, the pressure to perform is immense and I regularly had to check my motives. Why was I doing what I was doing? This all changed for me one day at a meeting in Bethel Church, Redding, California. I went along to a conference there as a delegate, just to receive whatever God had for me. There He began to do a deep work in my heart. The Father showed me some hurts that I had buried deep within and put His finger on them to heal me. He also showed me times in my ministry where I had simply relied on my gift, without waiting to hear His heart on a particular situation.

In the midst of receiving a deep deliverance from these past hurts and mistakes, God spoke to my heart so clearly and said,

"Son, I want you to grow up and become a child!"

These words undid me. I realised that the only posture one can assume in the Kingdom of God is that of childlikeness. I had lost my childlike awe and wonder at being adopted by the Father and immersed in His love.

Life can inflict many wounds on us, and it is easy to lose our focus, but we all need to come back to this: to revel in our adoption into sonship; to have our awe and wonder in our Father restored; most of all to embrace the incredible gift and promise that God has bestowed on us – the kiss of the Father. It is all by His Spirit!

Chapter 3

Convicting and Conforming

"Nevertheless, I tell you the truth: it is to your advantage
that I go away, for if I do not go away, the Helper will not
come to you. But if I go, I will send him to you. And when
he comes, he will convict the world concerning sin and
righteousness and judgment: concerning sin, because they
do not believe in me; concerning righteousness, because I
go to the Father, and you will see me no longer; concerning
judgment, because the ruler of this world is judged."
(John 16:7-11 ESV)

I remember it so well. I was sitting in church one morning
racked with nerves as the prophet at the front called various
people out. The details were staggering. Of course, I knew the
people he was prophesying over (though he didn't) and every
aspect was right, razor sharp in fact. Why was I so nervous?
I was utterly convinced that not only would I be singled out,
but that the Holy Spirit was going to use this man to paint a

grand picture for all to see. My sins and failings were about to be made public!

Thankfully, the opposite happened. I was indeed singled out, but the prophecy I received that morning gloriously revealed the heart of God to me. That's how the gifts of the Spirit are supposed to work – they are intended to build us up and encourage us. I had gotten the wrong idea, like so many Christians who get the verses at the beginning of this chapter in a muddle.

As a pastor, I would often have people in my office who had come for counselling. Sins would be confessed and repentance demonstrated, but despite praying with people and assuring them of the Father's forgiveness, I saw many who just could not shake off their guilt and shame. I saw believers who, though they professed to have embraced God's grace, lived like they were no better than a worm in the grass.

It seems to me that the reason for such personal recrimination is a fundamental misunderstanding of the role of the Holy Spirit with regard to the believer.

I believe many are not reading the Scriptures through the lens of a forgiven soul. The result is a focus on sin more than grace, and a preoccupation with our old, sinful past. One only needs to listen to the some of the songs that have come out of the contemporary Christian music scene to understand how often they are focussed on our pre-salvation state. This is understandable – we were sinners, evil-doers, God-rebels – but all of that changed at salvation.

"I have been crucified with Christ. It is no longer I who live, but Christ who lives in me. And the life I now live in the flesh I live by faith in the Son of God, who loved me and gave himself for me." (Galatians 2:20)

In Romans 8:14-15 we read,

"For all who are led by the Spirit of God are sons of God. For you did not receive the spirit of slavery to fall back into fear, but you have received the Spirit of adoption as sons, by whom we cry, Abba! Father!"

The standing before God of the person who has come to Christ is completely different than it used to be. In Christ, we die to the sin of the world, are buried with Him, are raised up in Him, ascended into heaven with Him, and are now seated with Him in heavenly places. This process began with the Holy Spirit convicting us about our sin and highlighting our desperate need for Jesus and His finished work on the cross.

Notice that John 16:8-10 says,

"And when [the Holy Spirit] comes, he will convict the world concerning sin and righteousness and judgment: concerning sin, because they do not believe in me; concerning righteousness, because I go to the Father, and you will see me no longer..." (ESV)

John writes that the Holy Spirit convicts the world concerning sin, "because they do not believe in me". The Holy Spirit doesn't just come to tell us we've done wrong, He convicts us when we are unsaved of our unbelief and convinces us to trust Jesus.

Most preaches I have heard on this text have had to do with general sin and how the Holy Spirit will make us feel bad, so that we'll know when we're about to do something wrong – or have already done it. But this is not the role of the Spirit in relation to the verses in John 16. Here He is clearly calling sinners to a place of faith and trust in Jesus' finished work.

The text goes on to say that the Spirit convicts the world regarding righteousness. As NT Wright in his commentary *John for Everyone*, points out: the Holy Spirit will "convict the world that God has decided in favour of Jesus as the righteous one. All those who follow Jesus share that verdict." Notice that Jesus says, "I go to the father and you will see me no longer." His righteousness, declared by the Father, is for our benefit. The Holy Spirit continually affirms this truth: we are righteous in every way that He is! This is a promise given to followers of Jesus as a continual reminder of who and whose they are. Jesus' words here underline that His vindication as righteous before the Father will come as gift to us by the Spirit when He is gone, The Spirit, whom the world cannot receive! The Holy Spirit comes to remind believers who we are, not who we were! He tells us about our right standing with the Father because Jesus went ahead to make a way for us. The outpouring of His Spirit reminds us of our rightness with God. Sin has been far removed. Holy Spirit affirms our sonship and tells us we are righteous. Herein lies the key to walking in holiness.

For most of my early Christian life I had a secret fear of the Holy Spirit because of the fire and brimstone sermons that abounded, saying that if we didn't listen to Him we would end up with a similar fate to Ananias and Sapphira. Sad to say, the teaching was so full of legalistic thinking that I never understood how kind and gentle the Holy Spirit is.

Some will protest at this point: *Are you saying that the Holy Spirit does not convict believers of sin?* Yes, that is exactly what I'm saying! After coming to Christ, He now convicts me of who I am in light of the cross. People find the message of grace hard to swallow because of its implications. *You mean I can sin whenever I want, without consequences, and the Holy Spirit will stand by and watch?* Of course not. If your predisposition is to see how much sin you can get away with, something is very wrong already!

Grace is not about what we can get away with, it's about what we get to enjoy now that we have found right standing with the Father. The Holy Spirit teaches us to say no to sin, because children of God don't behave that way. He doesn't do this by clobbering us every time we mess up, He does it by reminding us we are children of the King and should act according to our royal heritage.

The apostle Paul took the same approach. Much of his teaching focuses on helping us understand our post-salvation position in Christ, so that we realise we are no longer under any compulsion to sin. Writing to the church at Corinth – a place where so much glory and sin coexisted – Paul lists the sins of the past then says,

"And such were some of you. But you were washed, you were sanctified, you were justified in the name of the Lord Jesus Christ and by the Spirit of our God." (1 Corinthians 6:11)

Thank God for the word BUT! We'd all be dead in the water without that word.

Who we are in Christ

I want us to focus on who we are in Christ, so below I have listed some of the many verses that remind us of our identity in Him. They are all taken from the Amplified Bible (yes, they are a bit louder that way!). Meditate on these scriptures and allow yourself to become saturated in the truth of God's Word.

"All are justified and made upright and in right standing with God, freely and gratuitously by His grace (His unmerited favour and mercy), through the redemption which is [provided] in Christ Jesus." (Romans 3:24)

"Even so consider yourselves also dead to sin and your relation to it broken, but alive to God [living in unbroken fellowship with Him] in Christ Jesus." (Romans 6:11)

"Therefore, [there is] now no condemnation (no adjudging guilty of wrong) for those who are in Christ Jesus, who live [and] walk not after the dictates of the flesh, but after the dictates of the Spirit." (Romans 8:1)

"For the law of the Spirit of life [which is] in Christ Jesus [the law of our new being] has freed me from the law of sin and of death." (Romans 8:2)

"To the church (assembly) of God which is in Corinth, to those consecrated and purified and made holy in Christ Jesus, [who are] selected and called to be saints (God's people), together with all those who in any place call upon and give honour to the name of our Lord Jesus Christ, both their Lord and ours." (1 Corinthians 1:2)

"For just as [because of their union of nature] in Adam all people die, so also [by virtue of their union of nature] shall all in Christ be made alive." (1 Corinthians 15:22)

"But it is God Who confirms and makes us steadfast and establishes us [in joint fellowship] with you in Christ, and has consecrated and anointed us [enduing us with the gifts of the Holy Spirit]." (2 Corinthians 1:21)

"But thanks be to God, Who in Christ always leads us in triumph [as trophies of Christ's victory] and through us spreads and makes evident the fragrance of the knowledge of God everywhere." (2 Corinthians 2:14)

"Therefore if any person is [ingrafted] in Christ (the Messiah) he is a new creation (a new creature altogether); the old [previous moral and spiritual condition] has passed away. Behold, the fresh and new has come!" (2 Corinthians 5:17)

"[My precaution was] because of false brethren who had been secretly smuggled in [to the Christian brotherhood]; they had slipped in to spy on our liberty and the freedom which we have in Christ Jesus, that they might again bring us into bondage [under the Law of Moses]." (Galatians 2:4)

"For in Christ Jesus you are all sons of God through faith." (Galatians 3:26)

"There is [now no distinction] neither Jew nor Greek, there is neither slave nor free, there is not male and female; for you are all one in Christ Jesus." (Galatians 3:28)

"For [if we are] in Christ Jesus, neither circumcision nor uncircumcision counts for anything, but only faith activated

and energised and expressed and working through love."
(Galatians 5:6)

"May blessing (praise, laudation, and eulogy) be to the God
and Father of our Lord Jesus Christ (the Messiah) Who has
blessed us in Christ with every spiritual (given by the Holy
Spirit) blessing in the heavenly realm!" (Ephesians 1:3)

"Even as [in His love] He chose us [actually picked us out
for Himself as His own] in Christ before the foundation of the
world, that we should be holy (consecrated and set apart for
Him) and blameless in His sight, even above reproach, before
Him in love." (Ephesians 1:4)

"And He raised us up together with Him and made us
sit down together [giving us joint seating with Him] in the
heavenly sphere [by virtue of our being] in Christ Jesus (the
Messiah, the Anointed One)." (Ephesians 2:6)

"He did this that He might clearly demonstrate through the
ages to come the immeasurable (limitless, surpassing) riches
of His free grace (His unmerited favour) in [His] kindness and
goodness of heart toward us in Christ Jesus." (Ephesians 2:7)

"For we are God's [own] handiwork (His workmanship),
recreated in Christ Jesus, [born anew] that we may do those
good works which God predestined (planned beforehand) for
us [taking paths which He prepared ahead of time], that we
should walk in them [living the good life which He prearranged
and made ready for us to live]." (Ephesians 2:10)

"[It is this:] that the Gentiles are now to be fellow heirs [with the Jews], members of the same body and joint partakers [sharing] in the same divine promise in Christ through [their acceptance of] the glad tidings (the Gospel)." (Ephesians 3:6)

"And God's peace [shall be yours, that tranquil state of a soul assured of its salvation through Christ, and so fearing nothing from God and being content with its earthly lot of whatever sort that is, that peace] which transcends all understanding shall garrison and mount guard over your hearts and minds in Christ Jesus." (Philippians 4:7)

"I have strength for all things in Christ Who empowers me [I am ready for anything and equal to anything through Him Who infuses inner strength into me; I am self-sufficient in Christ's sufficiency]." (Philippians 4:13)

"And my God will liberally supply (fill to the full) your every need according to His riches in glory in Christ Jesus." (Philippians 4:19)

"Him we preach and proclaim, warning and admonishing everyone and instructing everyone in all wisdom comprehensive insight into the ways and purposes of God), that we may present every person mature (full-grown, fully initiated, complete, and perfect) in Christ (the Anointed One)." (Colossians 1:28)

"Thank [God] in everything [no matter what the circumstances may be, be thankful and give thanks], for this is the will of God for you [who are] in Christ Jesus [the Revealer and Mediator of that will]." (1 Thessalonians 5:18)

"And the grace (unmerited favour and blessing) of our Lord [actually] flowed out superabundantly and beyond measure for me, accompanied by faith and love that are [to be realised] in Christ Jesus." (1 Timothy 1:14)

"[For it is He] Who delivered and saved us and called us with a calling in itself holy and leading to holiness [to a life of consecration, a vocation of holiness]; [He did it] not because of anything of merit that we have done, but because of and to further His own purpose and grace (unmerited favour) which was given us in Christ Jesus before the world began [eternal ages ago]." (2 Timothy 1:9)

"Hold fast and follow the pattern of wholesome and sound teaching which you have heard from me, in [all] the faith and love which are [for us] in Christ Jesus." (2 Timothy 1:13)

"So you, my son, be strong (strengthened inwardly) in the grace (spiritual blessing) that is [to be found only] in Christ Jesus." (2 Timothy 2:1)

"And how from your childhood you have had a knowledge of and been acquainted with the sacred Writings, which are able to instruct you and give you the understanding for salvation which comes through faith in Christ Jesus [through the leaning of the entire human personality on God in Christ Jesus in absolute trust and confidence in His power, wisdom, and goodness]." (2 Timothy 3:15)

"And after you have suffered a little while, the God of all grace [Who imparts all blessing and favour], Who has called you to His [own] eternal glory in Christ Jesus, will Himself complete and make you what you ought to be, establish and ground you securely, and strengthen, and settle you." (1 Peter 5:10)

I hope you have given yourself sufficient time to just dwell on these incredible truths about your position in Christ and standing before our Almighty Father. What Jesus has done for us is truly incredible! And this is why the Holy Spirit, working in our lives to bring about inner transformation, is more interested in helping us conform to the likeness of Jesus than He is in convicting us of our sin.

It is through knowing and meditating on who we are in Christ that causes us to become like Him. If you were to examine your life through a spiritual microscope you would find that you struggle in certain areas because of a distorted view of your identity in Christ. This has been Satan's strategy from the beginning: to mislead us, to distort our view of who we are, to distort our view of who God is and our relationship to Him, to try to bring division. The evil one seeks to warp our identity in order to bring us under the bondage of sin.

Adam and Eve fell because Satan distorted the character of God, insinuating that He was withholding something good from them, which was a complete lie. Then Adam and Eve became confused about their own identity – they forgot that they already were "like God", because they were made in His image.

Where Adam and Eve failed, Jesus won the test of temptation. After being affirmed by His Father as the Son of God, the devil immediately tried to challenge His identity as a son in order to lead him into temptation. Again the enemy tried to distort the goodness of the Father and the identity of His Son!

Think about an example in your own life. For instance, say a person worries about not having enough resources to live on. As a child of God, the Father has promised to meet all of their needs. He is committed to providing for them, both naturally and supernaturally. Yet this is still an issue for them. Why? It is because they still have "trust issues" with God – they don't quite believe that He will provide for all their needs. This is due to a distortion of identity. Either the Father's identity is in question: is He *really* committed to providing for my needs? Or, their own identity is in question: am I really a royal child of God, who should expect their needs to be met? Do I *really* deserve that?

You can see how the enemy's lies rob us of so much! The trouble is, we have orientated our lives around our old sinful nature, viewing ourselves through an unregenerate lens. We can't use that lens any more, because we have been made new creatures in Christ! Jesus has restored our relationship with the Father and He wants us to trust Him; to trust in His goodness towards us.

Religion has painted a picture of a God who is angry, demanding, capricious and a killjoy. Nothing could be further from the truth! On the contrary, because of the cross we are now privileged to enter into an intimate relationship with Him full of grace, mercy, peace and joy.

We need to ask the Lord to renew our minds. The principle of Scripture is "as a man thinks, so is he". In other words, whatever we behold we become. Which is why it is so important that we cultivate an intimate personal relationship with the Holy Spirit. He is the one who helps us behold Jesus in all His glory and so become more like Him.

"Now the Lord is the Spirit, and where the Spirit of the Lord is, there is freedom. And we all, with unveiled face, beholding the glory of the Lord, are being transformed into the same image from one degree of glory to another. For this comes from the Lord who is the Spirit." (2 Corinthians 3:17-18)

Chapter 4

He is Power

My dad is one of my heroes. He is a man of faith, full of the Spirit and there is no guile in him. I have always loved hearing him speak about his salvation – how he got saved in the midst of a great family tragedy as God in His grace stepped into the situation.

My older sister, Janice (I never got the chance to meet her) was struggling with a severe heart condition that eventually took her life. Dad recalls that one of the nurses, who had taken a liking to Janice, had such a sense of peace about her. Hearing her pray for my sister, Dad just knew that God was listening to her. Her spirituality intrigued Dad and he began asking questions about Jesus. Jesus broke into Dad's life and he gave his heart to Him. Never underestimate the effect your faith has on others in the workplace! However seemingly insignificant you believe your role to be, you can actually have a massive influence on others.

Dad later connected with a bunch of radical Pentecostals – and Pentecostal theology places a large emphasis on a second experience of the Holy Spirit, following on from salvation, known as the "baptism in the Holy Spirit". It urges believers to continue to pursue God, after salvation, and to press in for this latter infilling, citing speaking in tongues as the primary evidence of the experience.

According to his reading of Scripture, looking at the examples found in the book of Acts, Dad knew that he wanted to be baptised in the Spirit, but it did not go well for him. After numerous attempts at praying and then trying to speak in tongues, he was left disappointed and frustrated.

Two years later he was in a Baptist church where the pastor spoke simply and clearly about the nature of God as our Father, referring to the promise of Luke 11 – that he who asks for a good gift will receive it from the Lord. Hearing this, Dad realised that God would not have withheld the Holy Spirit from him when he asked, so therefore he must have received Him. As soon as he had processed this revelation it was like flicking a switch and he began to speak in tongues. More than that, in Dad's own words, "When I received this wonderful gift from the Father, my desire to serve Jesus exploded. I wanted to preach the Word and I knew I was called to serve the Church. My values changed and I saw life in a whole new light."

I have seen the fruit of his experience and of the on going communion Dad has with the Holy Spirit. He is a natural soul winner and I don't know any other person who has had such significant breakthroughs as him when leading others into the baptism in the Spirit. His passion for Jesus, his worship and his service have never waned – he is such a great role model to me!

My own experience of being filled with the Holy Spirit was an overwhelming one. Waves of joy washed over me and I wanted to bounce up and down as His power surged through me. It was, at once, both exhilarating and frightening! Like my dad, things changed for me afterwards as my priorities in life were radically changed.

In his book The Spirit filled Church, Terry Virgo recounts how he was filled with the Spirit: "As I relaxed it was as if a flood of the Holy Spirit went right through me. I found myself not only speaking freely in tongues, but also calling out to God in the most loving and intimate terms that I could not imagine. God was right in my heart! His love was absolutely overflowing in me! I truly loved Him like never before."

Not everyone has a dramatic experience like this when they are filled with the Holy Spirit, others may receive Him in gentle quietness, but this does not mean they are not being filled to overflowing!

How and when?

For years the how and when of receiving the baptism of the Holy Spirit has been debated by theologians, with many differing opinions, and the questions still on the lips of many are: *"How do I get it?"* and *"When do I get it?"*

Many books have been written on the subject of the baptism of the Spirit and it is not my purpose here to take an in-depth look at the different theological arguments surrounding the topic – but I do want to make a couple of observations.

First of all, I want to make clear that I believe a person

receives the Holy Spirit at conversion. It is impossible not to, since the Holy Spirit is the one who leads us to Christ. The fact that the Holy Spirit indwells us is the main distinction between the New Covenant and the Old. Under the Old Covenant the Holy Spirit rested on a person for a season, imparting a powerful enabling for living, for a time – but this was only a temporary measure. For example, the Spirit came on Samson to give him power to defeat the Philistines (Judges 14:6,19). Under the New Covenant, however, God comes to dwell and remain in us, by His Spirit.

"Do you not know that you are God's temple and that God's Spirit dwells in you?" (1 Corinthians 3:16)

Theologians who argue against the baptism of the Spirit as an event separate from salvation tend to use 1 Corinthians 12:13 as a proof text:

"For in one Spirit we were all baptized into one body—Jews or Greeks, slaves[a] or free—and all were made to drink of one Spirit."

In his book Holy Fire, Dr RT Kendall writes that, "to superimpose Luke's usage of the baptism with the Holy Spirit upon 1 Corinthians 12:3 – and to claim that all Christians automatically experience what the early church experienced – is incongruous. Paul is not saying all Christians receive the baptism with the Holy Spirit (as describe by Luke in the book of Acts) at conversion. Certainly not."

My understanding of the Holy Spirit as a second experience has to do with the Holy Spirit coming upon a person and anointing them with power – an experience that both witnesses to our adoption as children of God and equips and empowers us for mission.

Although the phrase "the baptism of the Spirit" appears infrequently in Scripture, the biblical principles and examples are clear. In Acts 2 we see the outpouring of the Spirit, which empowers the disciples after they have been saved. Acts 8:14-16 describes how, having heard that a new group of believers had "received the word of the Lord" in Samaria, the apostles sent Peter and John to pray for them, "so that they might receive the Holy Spirit, for he had not yet fallen on any of them … they had only been baptized in the name of the Lord Jesus."

Again, in Acts 19:1-7, we read that Paul, having come across some believers on his travels in Ephesus, asks them, "Did you receive the Holy Spirit when you believed?" The men reply, "No, we have not even heard that there is a Holy Spirit." Subsequently, Paul prays for them: "And when Paul had laid his hands on them, the Holy Spirit came on them, and they began speaking in tongues and prophesying." The point is, Paul didn't assume that new believers automatically received the empowering touch of the Holy Spirit at conversion – it was a later experience.

Some will argue that one shouldn't try to build a theological argument on "narrative" bits of Scripture, but I think this is an unhelpful way of looking at the Bible, which speaks about itself saying, "All scripture is God-breathed and useful for instruction." (2 Timothy 3:16).

What are the results?
What are the results of baptism in the Spirit? It is clear to me, both from my reading of Scripture and my experience, that the baptism of the Spirit is about moving from sonship

to empowerment for service. The baptism results in empowered witness – and this is not a one-time operation, but the Holy Spirit continues to fill us to overflowing – there are further encounters which God uses to irrevocably change the believer, producing joy, spiritual power, boldness and an outflow of spiritual gifts.

My own encounter with the Holy Spirit moved me from being a shy, introverted young man into a bold preacher of the Word. I also spoke in other tongues. Tongues is a very important aspect of the Christian life, which I believe every believer can and should have and use. It is one of the most underrated gifts God has given His Church, yet it remains a contentious issue for many.

Although I believe that one can flow in the gifts of the Spirit without ever speaking in tongues, I have found that tongues is frequently the "gateway gift" to all the other expressions of the Holy Spirit. We will discuss this in detail in chapter 8 and if you don't currently speak in tongues, but want to, there is a prayer you can pray in the appendix of this book.

Phenomena of power have always accompanied the works of the Holy Spirit – something which, again, has proven to be controversial for some believers. Both Scripture and Christian history document numerous example of the Holy Spirit breaking out with signs and wonders – much of which does not sit well with our intellect-dominated society, where people try to compartmentalise everything and nothing can be believed unless one can work out a formula for it.

I am not arguing against not using our intellects, it's just that our limited minds cannot fully comprehend God, and the Holy Spirit will often supersede our intellect.

Manifestations of the Spirit's power

Some sections of the Church, whilst not denying the baptism of the Spirit, argue that it no longer happens today and state that, in the past, the Holy Spirit came due to exceptional circumstances.

I have also heard people say things like, "God only does miracles to prove His existence in developing world contexts. The West has the Bible, so we don't need miracles as much."

The traditional cessationist viewpoint is that the Holy Spirit was poured out in Acts purely to help establish the Church — and that we should no longer expect such phenomena because we have matured.

But the evidence is there to show that both the work and phenomena of the Holy Spirit have continued throughout the Church age. For example, Ireneaus (an early Church father discipled by Polycarp, who himself was discipled by the Apostle John), wrote in his book Against Heresies, about the Holy Spirit phenomena the Church continued to experience:

"Some do certainly and truly drive out devils, so that those who have thus been cleansed from evil spirits frequently both believe (in Christ) and join themselves to the church. Others have foreknowledge of things to come, they see visions, and utter prophetic expressions. Others still, heal the sick by laying their hands upon them, and they are made whole. Yea, moreover, as I have said, the dead even have been raised up, and remained among us for many years. And what shall I more say? It is not possible to name the number of the gifts which the church, (scattered) throughout the whole world, has received from God, in the name of Jesus Christ."

I have had the privilege of ministering in France on many

occasions and particularly in the Huguenot region of southern France, where there have been incredible outpourings of the Holy Spirit. The Huguenots were protestants who came into an experience of the Spirit during the 1500-1700s and history records stories of "laughing preachers" and "ecstatic trances". John Cabanel of Anduze wrote about it in his day and is quoted in the book Miracles and Manifestations of the Holy Spirit in the History of the Church by Jeff Doles:

"Several of those persons I saw violently agitated; during the inspiration they had great shakings of the whole body, motions of the head, the arm and the breast; their exhortations to repentance were urgent, and they assured that God would shortly destroy Babylon ... I heard many of those after the inspiration ceased say they could not repeat the things they had said in it..."

People often ask if such manifestations can be found in Scripture. Here I quote Dr Gary Greig, who wrote answering critics of the Lakeland Florida outpouring:

"Let's ask the same questions about the biblical evidence that the critics are asking about ... the Lakeland outpouring: was it weird or unbiblical for Ezekiel to fall over in the Lord's presence when the glory of God was manifesting where he was (Ezekiel 1:28; 2:23)? Or was it weird and unbiblical for Daniel to fall over and tremble and shake in the presence of the angel of the Lord (Daniel 10:8-11)? The following passages suggest it is normal to tremble and shake in the Lord's presence:

Psalm 114:7: 'Tremble, O earth, at the presence of the Lord.'
Jeremiah 5:22: 'Should you not tremble in my presence?'
Or was it weird and unbiblical for Jeremiah's bones to

shake, vibrate and tremble and for him to stumble around awkwardly in a drunken state, 'because of the Lord and his holy words' (Jeremiah 23:9)?

Was it weird for Saul, when the Spirit came upon him in Naioth at Ramah, to strip off his outer clothes and lay down 'prophesying' for a whole day and night (1 Samuel 19:23-24)? Was it weird and unbiblical for John to fall over 'in the Spirit' when Christ appeared to him (Revelation 1:10, 17), or for Paul to fall on the road to Damascus (Acts 9:4; 26:11), or for the soldiers and officials to fall before Jesus in the Garden (John 18:6)?

Was it weird and unbiblical for believers to stagger about, intoxicated by the Holy Spirit's presence and power in Acts 2 (Acts 2:4, 13, 15)? The answer is obviously no, but such phenomena clearly happened when the Spirit of the Lord became manifest in glorious power, according to Scripture."

The manifestation of the Holy Spirit's power – and physical responses to that power – are commonplace in the Bible and should be in today's Church. Many, including myself, testify to a deeper revelation of God's goodness and a deeper love for Scripture following the infilling of the Spirit. The Holy Spirit is power and I pray for each of us to encounter Him more powerfully today!

Chapter 5

The Christ Anointing

"And the Spirit of the Lord shall rest upon him."
(Isaiah 11:2)

Jesus was recognised by His anointing

John the Baptiser was born into promise. He was blessed with an anointing of the Holy Spirit from a young age and had a specific calling on his life: to prepare the way for the Messiah. His job was to help people to recognise and receive the one who would usher in the shalom of Yahweh. Many prophecies had been recorded about the one on whom the Christ anointing would rest and it was John's privilege to identify him.

God had promised that in the place where man had lost the joy and intimacy of fellowship with Him, He would raise one up who would crush the serpent's head and deal with all the illegitimate authority of the imposing spiritual powers. He would be born from the womb of a woman and He would carry a heavenly DNA to break the curse that blighted mankind.

For many years the people of God had awaited the coming of the Messiah, also known as Emmanuel, "God with us", the one who would deliver the people Yahweh. They were waiting for the one who would make all things new again and restore God's kingdom – simply known as, the Christ.

The name "Christ" summed up the revelation of who Jesus was and what He was called to do. Jesus Christ means "Jesus, the anointed one" and this is how John was to recognise Him – the Spirit would come upon Him and remain upon Him.

When I was growing up, the terminology used in our church was the "unction of the Spirit". Unction simply means the act of anointing. But unlike those in the Bible who knew a moment of unction, Jesus would know the continued, abiding anointing of the Spirit throughout His life on earth.

Today not many Christians talk about the anointing and I believe there is a great deal of confusion about how that term relates to us. Let's explore what it means.

We receive the same anointing as Jesus

The Old Covenant foreshadowed the anointing of the Holy Spirit by demonstrating a physical representation of an inner work. Priests, and later prophets and kings, were set apart for ministry to God and His people by being publically anointed with oil. The Chief Priest would take a horn of oil and pour it over the head of the priest/prophet/king to be. It was a physical enactment of a spiritual reality – of the person being set aside to serve God, and of being cleansed, filled and empowered for ministry.

The act of anointing represented the coming of the Holy

Spirit, but since the New Covenant, Jesus anoints His followers with His Spirit, poured out. The word "Christian" is derived from the Greek word Christos, which itself is a translation of the Hebrew word mashiach, meaning "anointed one".

In other words, we are anointed by the Anointed One. We get the very same anointing that Jesus Himself received at His baptism. That is why we are called Christians – because we are "little Christs". The presence of the Holy Spirit has come to rest on us. We are in Christ and He is in us – that is the beauty of this supernatural union! My oneness with Christ is the work of the Holy Spirit. The power of the Holy Spirit is given to us in order that Christ might dwell in us (Ephesians 3:16-19).

R. A. Torrey speaks about the role of the Holy Spirit to transform us from the inside out:

"It is the work of the Holy Spirit to form the living Christ within us, dwelling deep down in the depths of our being. We have already seen that this was part of the significance of the name sometimes used of the Holy Spirit, 'the Spirit of Christ.' In Christ on the cross of Calvary, made an atoning sacrifice for sin, bearing the curse of the broken law in our place, we have Christ for us. But by the power of the Holy Spirit bestowed on us by the risen Christ we have Christ in us. Herein lies the secret of a Christlike life."

The secret of a Christlike life is to recognise that all we do, we do by the Spirit and not out of our own resources!

It is the paradox known theologically as the hypostatic union that Jesus was at once, fully man and fully God. Much has been said about how Jesus overcame temptation, performed His miracles, and went through the process of death and resurrection. Without getting into a debate about the hypostatic union, it is clear that orthodox Christianity affirms the fact that Jesus lived a fully human life and experienced the full range of human emotions and challenges without ever ceasing to be God.

However, until His baptism, Jesus didn't experience the anointing of the Holy Spirit and wasn't recognised as the Christ. This is important for us to realise, because just as Jesus lived a power-filled life, under the anointing of the Spirit, so too can we. We are invited to receive the same anointing.

A. B. Simpson, in his commentary, The Holy Spirit, says, "[Jesus] was truly the eternal God, very God, of very God. But when He came down from yonder heights of glory He suspended the direct operation of His own independent power and became voluntarily dependent upon the power of God through the Holy Ghost ... He purposely took His place side by side with us, heeding equally with the humblest disciple the constant power of God to sustain Him in all His work ... And so He went through life in the position of dependence, that He might be our public example and teach us that we too have the same secret of strength and power that He possessed, and that as surely as He overcame through the Holy Ghost, so may we."

Similarly, Gerald Hawthorne in his book, The Presence and The Power, presses the point:

"Not only is Jesus their Saviour because of who he was and because of his own complete obedience to the Father's will (cf. Hebrews 10:5-7), but he is the supreme example for them of what is possible in a human life because of his own total dependence upon the Spirit of God. Jesus is living proof of how those who are his followers may exceed the limitations of their humanness in order that they, like him, might carry to completion against all odds their God-given mission in life – by the Holy Spirit. Jesus demonstrated clearly that God's intended way for human beings to live, the ideal way to live, the supremely successful way to live, is in conjunction with God, in harmony with God, in touch with the power of God, and not apart from God, not independent of God, not without God. The Spirit was the presence and power of God in Jesus, and fully so."

Theologian Dr Sam Storms summed it up very simply in a recent article on his website: "It was not primarily by virtue of his divine nature that Jesus lived the kind of life he did, but rather through his constant and ever increasing reliance on the Holy Spirit."

Weakness and humility – keys to the anointing

It's interesting that Jesus Himself went through the waters of baptism. John's baptism was a baptism of repentance, yet Jesus had no sin to repent of. But Jesus was willing to identify Himself with mankind and so humbled Himself by receiving John's baptism. Humility is a key to receiving the anointing.

Whilst we are picturing this scene of Jesus being baptised in the Jordan river, let me make one further observation. Something prophetic is happening here. Jesus is baptised at the same river where the people of God crossed over into the Promised Land. Jesus' baptism pointed towards the promise of abundant life, needs met, victories won. The Jordan represented Israel's longings and desires. When Jesus was being baptised He Himself was entering into that promise, which comes to us by the Spirit. The abundant life of the age to come was finally breaking in. Heaven was touching earth again!

Isaiah's prophecy concerning the coming Messiah speaks at length about the role of the Holy Spirit and how His anointing would be outworked in Jesus' life:

"There shall come forth a shoot from the stump of Jesse, and a branch from his roots shall bear fruit. And the Spirit of the LORD shall rest upon him, the Spirit of wisdom and understanding, the Spirit of counsel and might, the Spirit of knowledge and the fear of the LORD. And his delight shall be in the fear of the LORD. He shall not judge by what his eyes see, or decide disputes by what his ears hear, but with righteousness he shall judge the poor, and decide with equity for the meek of the earth; and he shall strike the earth with the rod of his mouth, and with the breath of his lips he shall kill the wicked. Righteousness shall be the belt of his waist, and faithfulness the belt of his loins." (Isaiah 11:1-5)

Isaiah's prophecy points to the future when the one carrying the Christ-anointing will finally release God's rule and reign on the earth. Jesus would come to establish God's Kingdom as the greatest kingdom over all the earth.

This Scripture sums up the posture we need to adopt in order to enjoy the full work of the Spirit in our lives. Jesus is described as a tiny shoot of life springing from an already withered stump. The picture is one of extreme weakness and vulnerability. It wouldn't take much to destroy a new shoot that was emerging. Such vulnerability almost seems unwise, yet it is an amazing display of God's mysterious wisdom.

Later, Isaiah will speak of Jesus as a "bruised reed" and

"smouldering flame". It is God's wisdom to use what seems weak, foolish, even useless to others and use it to confound the so-called wise. The resting place of the Holy Spirit is not with what the world deems "suitable" or powerful. God is amazing. He anointed an uneducated carpenter from a sketchy background in a town most people ignored and made Him the centrepiece of mankind's salvation and redemption! No wonder it was offensive to the Pharisees of Jesus' day.

Weakness is a key to the anointing. There is strength in acknowledging that we are not able to do things for ourselves; that we need God's help in all things. These are the qualifications we need for the Spirit's anointing to flow in our lives.

Kathryn Kuhlman used to say, "God is not looking for golden vessels; He is not looking for silver vessels; God is looking for yielded vessels." Our availability qualifies us to be used by God, but the degree of our humility and weakness are the factors that determine how much God can use us to accomplish His purposes.

God has given me the privilege of serving Him through the prophetic ministry and people often comment that I am able to prophesy with great clarity, accuracy and power. You would think that to be able to stand in front of a crowd of people and deliver such prophetic words would point to a life that is powerful and confident – but nothing could be further from the truth.

As a preacher, I can't point to any major diplomas or degrees I have hanging on my study wall. It's not that I'm against study or training – I just don't have those qualifications! During my formative school years I was one of a class of 49 pupils.

Parents and teachers alike will know that learning in such a large group doesn't tend to hone high academic habits and skills.

Then I was born prematurely with Pierre Robin Syndrome – a cleft palate is one of its common characteristics – which severely impacted my speech. Added to this, for most of my childhood I had a sickly constitution.

All of this affected me in social settings. I was deeply shy and had a fear of crowds. At school, I dreaded any project that included a class presentation, where I was expected to get up and speak in front of my classmates. I would literally be sick beforehand. In fact, my entire school experience was marred by the ridicule of my peers. Their harsh words pierced me deeply and exacerbated my speech impediment and general awkwardness.

In an earlier chapter I made reference to an occasion when a pastor singled me out in a meeting. I was worried about my "secret sin" being exposed, but instead the grace and goodness of God came flowing out. That pastor with a prophetic word was Louis Els, a pastor from Jeffrey's Bay, South Africa, who had been profoundly touched by the Father's Blessing that came out of Toronto in 1994 and swept across the world.

I was 15 years old and I remember Louis calling me out of the crowd and praying for me. It was a life-changing encounter. As Louis prayed, the Holy Spirit filled me with such "electric" power that I began to bounce up and down. I also began to laugh loudly – a deep, unrestrained belly laugh!

The only problem with the whole experience was that, up until then, I had been known as the "church mouse". It was so totally out of character that everyone was astonished, including me. Yet, it was the most exhilarating, powerful moment with God I'd experienced up until then. So profound was the change in me that the following week I preached my first sermon to our youth group and had a tangible sense of the Holy Spirit's anointing upon me.

I was so grateful to God. He had filled me with His power and transformed me. I knew then, if I hadn't known before, that He had a plan for my life that wildly exceeded all my expectations. Talk about God confounding the wise. He took a boy who had been ridiculed for his speech impediment and gave him a ministry of speech – preaching and uttering prophetic words!

God anointed my speech in order to build His kingdom. He took my weakest characteristic, the most insecure, vulnerable part of me, and made it the vehicle for His purposes. It is divine justice. God uses the weak to disarm the strong! Yay, God!

If God can do this for me, He can do it for you too. If you yield to God, He can take your weak flesh and do something extraordinary. Remember that Jesus only stepped into the miraculous after He was filled with the Holy Spirit. Until then he was simply a man who could do no miracles. If you had passed Him in the street, there would have been nothing remarkable about Him to make Him stand out (Isaiah 53:2). It was the coming of the Spirit that set Him apart. It was the Holy Spirit who empowered Him to live as the perfect second Adam! And therein lies and an incredible truth: the Holy Spirit reveals the Christ anointing. He is the one who releases, "Christ in you the hope of glory".

How did Jesus do what He did? How did the great pioneers of the Christian faith throughout history do what they did? It was the Christ anointing. The same power that fuelled Jesus' ministry, available to you and me, so that we can do even greater things than He did.

"I have been crucified with Christ. It is no longer I who live, but Christ who lives in me. And the life I now live in the flesh I live by faith in the Son of God, who loved me and gave himself for me." (Galatians 2:20)

"For all who are led by the Spirit of God are sons of God. For you did not receive the spirit of slavery to fall back into fear, but you have received the Spirit of adoption as sons, by whom we cry, Abba! Father!" (Romans 8:14)

Outbreak of the miraculous

The amazing thing about moving in the anointing is how, by cooperating with Him, the Holy Spirit will reveal truth and wisdom to us. Not just concerning Scripture, though He will give us a depth of revelation regarding biblical truth – but His truth and wisdom flow into everyday situations and circumstances. The Holy Spirit can speak to us about medical conditions or business ideas. Remember that He is all-knowing, so if we need to know something, all we have to do is ask!

The Holy Spirit is the best doctor, the best economist, the most well-equipped academic ever. He is our great teacher.

Recently, I prayed with a couple who desperately wanted a baby, but were struggling to conceive. The Holy Spirit gave me a word of knowledge regarding a medical condition that the lady had – something which had been misdiagnosed by her doctor. She went back to see her doctor, who realised his mistake and gave her appropriate treatment. Once this issue had been dealt with, she fell pregnant. I am no doctor, and I don't understand the workings of the female body, but the Holy Spirit knows everything and He can reveal to us what we need to know.

Similarly, I am often invited into businesses to pray for the business and its staff. In this context the Holy Spirit will often drop words into my mind that I have not learned; words that have special meaning for the business owners, such as "diversify" or "sequestration" – phrases that are not part of my day-to-day vocabulary. Speaking them has released the wisdom of heaven into business situations with a profound impact.

Qualities of the anointing

Isaiah's Messianic prophecy, mentioned earlier, gave insight into how Jesus would minister and what were the qualities of the anointing. It gives us guidance on how to move in the anointing of the Spirit and what we can expect:

- The anointing of the Holy Spirit come upon the believer, but also dwells within.
- It is both felt and recognised by others (Luke 5:17 says that the power of the Lord was present to heal.)
- The anointing is activated by faith (e.g. the woman with the blood disorder in Luke 8)
- The anointing operates in a context of joy (Hebrews 1:9 speaks of Jesus being anointed with joy and Hebrews 12 of the joy for which Jesus endured the cross)
- The Holy Spirit's anointing has a teaching element (1 John 3) – we are "shown" things that do not come by normal

information gathering, but by supernatural revelation.

- The anointing is released by honour. Jesus was inhibited in His work whilst in Nazareth, because of a lack of recognition and honour.
- The anointing empowers mission. The Holy Spirit comes to affirm our sonship, but also to release us into purpose – it is power with purpose, to fulfil the works God has called us to.
- The anointing is imparted. Jesus laid His hands on His disciples and His disciples on others. Similarly, we position ourselves to receive from God via impartation. It can happen when we're alone, but most often God uses the ministry of others and the laying on of hands (James 5) to impart the anointing.

These are just some of the characteristics of the anointing. Jesus modelled all of them to us and lived a life submitted to the Holy Spirit. We are called to do the same and to touch the world with the power of the Christ anointing.

Chapter 6
The Sevenfold Spirit

"And the Spirit of the LORD shall rest upon him, the Spirit of
wisdom and understanding, the Spirit of counsel and might,
the Spirit of knowledge and the fear of the LORD."
(Isaiah 11:2)

Four times in the book of Revelation we read the phrase "the
seven Spirits of God" or the "sevenfold Spirit of God". Biblical
scholars have classically interpreted these verses as referring
to the Holy Spirit and point back to Isaiah 11:2, which tells
us what are these seven characteristics of the Holy Spirit's
nature.

Without getting too crazy about the number 7, I do believe
we see some typology in the Old and New Testament's that
hint at the Holy Spirit's nature. In the Old Testament, the Holy
Spirit was the illuminating presence of God, represented by the
menorah — the seven-headed candle that was found in the tent
of meeting and wasn't allowed to be extinguished. It was the

priest's job to ensure that the flame continued to burn. In the New Testament, we see a similar picture of the Holy Spirit in Revelation – the seven lamps of fire which are the seven Spirits – or sevenfold Spirit – of God. In biblical terms, the number seven represents perfection or completion. We are sealed with the Holy Spirit at salvation because He completes us.

So Isaiah describes the Holy Spirit as the Spirit of:

1. The Lord
2. Wisdom
3. Understanding
4. Counsel
5. Might
6. Knowledge
7. The fear of the Lord

And he groups together closely related attributes, e.g. wisdom and understanding. Let's examine what each expression of the Spirit means for us.

The Spirit of the Lord

In verse two we see the first expression of the Holy Spirit as the Spirit of the Lord. With this expression, Isaiah identifies the Holy Spirit as the one who oversaw the creation of the world. Isaiah wants his readers to understand that the same Spirit who created the world is the same Spirit who, resting on the Messiah, will restore order and usher in the new earth. The poet-prophet Isaiah is intentionally employing imagery from Israel's history in order to help them understand their future.

It is worth mentioning here that the anointing in the Old Testament is most often connected to governmental offices.

Prophets, priests and kings carried the anointing of God for a season. When a king made a judicial decree, it was fulfilled simply because he said so. I believe that today the Lord is restoring our understanding of the creative force of the declared word. God's words in our mouths are as powerful as His words were in Jesus' mouth.

"The Spirit of the Lord" speaks of the divine presence and nature coming upon ordinary flesh and blood. The very force that was present in creation comes to empower us! When the Holy Spirit "speaks" into our life, a creative miracle happens – just as the Lord spoke at creation to create something that was not there. His word releases peace, power and authority; it brings things in order, the way God intended for them to be.

In Jesus' mission mandate, recorded in Isaiah 61:1-2, we read that part of His task on the earth is "to proclaim liberty to the captives". Jesus was anointed to "proclaim" – to speak out – and His proclamation brought about a breakout of God's kingdom.

George Eldon Ladd, in his book The Presence of the Future, says that in, "...the words Jesus said, in and of themselves, consisted power to accomplish that which it demanded." Jesus knew that His very words, spoken under the inspiration of the Spirit, contained the power to accomplish God's will. Notice that we never see Jesus praying that God the Father will heal the sick – He simply commands people to be healed.

When Jesus spoke to the man with the withered hand, He simply said, "Stretch out your hand." His words carried the power to restore the man's hand. When Jesus spoke to the woman caught in adultery and said, "Go and sin no more," He wasn't judging her, He was releasing her – it was an empowering word.

Once, on a trip to Clarens, South Africa, I was part of a group running a healing school and we prayed for many people. I prayed for one lady who'd had to have her kneecap surgically removed. After receiving prayer, the Lord grew a new kneecap for her.

On another occasion, after preaching at a church service, a young couple came for prayer. They wanted to be able to conceive, but the girl had serious gynaecological problems – she'd had one ovary removed and the other had been severely damaged due to a botched operation. Doctors gave her no hope of ever conceiving. We prayed and I commanded a new womb to be formed. In due course, she went into hospital for some scans and they revealed that not only was her damaged ovary completely healed, the one that had been removed had been supernaturally "recreated" and she had a perfectly healthy womb! This couple now have a little boy called Samuel.

I recall these stories not to make myself sound really spiritual or holy, but to illustrate the fact that God can and will use imperfect people to do amazing things and creative miracles can happen as we partner with the Spirit of the Lord.

The Spirit of wisdom and understanding

I mentioned briefly in the previous chapter that the Holy Spirit is the one who teaches us – and He is the best teacher! In the New Testament, teaching is not an intellectual exercise, but an experiential exercise, and one that always leads us into a deeper understanding of God's presence and glory. Any theology that does not lead us into an encounter with God simply makes us more religious.

The Spirit rested on Jesus to tutor Him and He desires to do the same for us. The Holy Spirit is an expert in everything. It doesn't matter what the issue is, He is the perfect teacher and the perfect helper! We need to lean on Him more and not try to figure things out with our own, earthly wisdom.

Spiritual wisdom and understanding are linked in Hebrew thinking. Wisdom is the reservoir from which understanding flows. As we cooperate with Him, the Holy Spirit teaches us to be wise, which helps us to rightly apply truth in every circumstance. More than this, wisdom here also refers to the ability to be skilfully creative.

Understanding is the power to see right into the heart of a matter and apply biblical truth to it. Jesus demonstrated both wisdom and understanding when the Pharisees tried to corner Him and trip Him up with their questions about doctrine. Jesus first discerned their motives before answering their objections.

When Jesus encountered the woman at the well, He was able to see past her façade and into her life, discerning where her life was at. As a result He was able to navigate her to a place of freedom. Wisdom and understanding go together. The Holy Spirit can break open to us that which is hidden, so that we can declare God's truth into a situation.

I often find that Holy Spirit gives me words for businessmen or politicians about complicated situations they are in. The Spirit helps us to get to the heart of the matter and apply His truth, so that it benefits the person receiving prayer and extends God's kingdom.

The Holy Spirit helps us to think like God and gives us insight into His heart:

"But, as it is written, What no eye has seen, nor ear heard, nor the heart of man imagined, what God has prepared for those who love him—these things God has revealed to us through the Spirit. For the Spirit searches everything, even the depths of God. For who knows a person's thoughts except the spirit of that person, which is in him? So also no one comprehends the thoughts of God except the Spirit of God. Now we have received not the spirit of the world, but the Spirit who is from God, that we might understand the things freely given us by God." (1 Corinthians 2:9-12)

What are the implications of this? We are privileged, by the Holy Spirit, to "tune in" to the heart and thoughts of God. It means that believers are uniquely privileged to receive insights that the world is desperate for. We have insight into truth that no one else has. We get to lead in creativity. It sets the Church apart for greatness and kingdom influence. It's how we extend God's rule in the earth.

The Spirit of counsel and might

Here Isaiah's words carry a sense of military ability. The Holy Spirit both counsels us – in the sense of an expert military strategist – and equips us with the power to accomplish that which is set before us; strategy and strength.

The Holy Spirit can unlock strategic plans for your individual destiny, for your relationships, for your work, for your local church, and more. Not only that, but He then supplies the might to accompany those plans – literally, the working of His power to fulfil them. In Galatians 3:5 Paul speaks about Jesus who "supplies the Spirit to you and works miracles among you...". The word "supplies" here means to provide something fully, covering all costs incurred. The word "might" in Isaiah carries exactly the same sense: the Holy Spirit gives us the strategy to do something, then He supplies all the resources to accomplish it.

I believe this is exactly what Jesus meant when He said, "I only do what I see my Father doing..." (John 5:19). He was attentive to the Spirit's counsel and then relied on the Spirit's power to release heaven's strategy onto the earth.

The Spirit of knowledge and the fear of the lord

The word "knowledge" here speaks of truth grasped and rightly applied to life, and also an awareness and understanding of the heart and nature of God. The Holy Spirit not only enables us to know what's right, He empowers us to live right, and He leads us into a deeper "knowing" of the Father.

The Holy Spirit seeks to bring us into intimacy. "Knowledge" is knowing God's heart and His ways, not through intellectual assent, but supernaturally, by His Spirit. Psalm 103 tells us that Israel knew the "acts of God", yet God "revealed His ways" to Moses.

So, as we continue to yield to the Holy Spirit in our life He increasingly reveals the heart and mind of God to us. This then is the basis for the fear of the Lord. We revere Him because we know Him. Reverential fear is an integral aspect of intimacy. It means that we treat our relationship with Jesus carefully and soberly. The Holy Spirit teaches us how to worship the Father and respond to His presence fearfully and joyfully. The Bible tells us that Jesus' mother, Mary, was both full of fear and joy. Both responses are appropriate at the same time!

When we are committed to walking in the Spirit's anointing,

the sense of the fear of the Lord can be tangible and other people notice it. Wherever Jesus went, the demonic reacted to the presence of God's Spirit and cried out. They couldn't help but respond to the fear of the Lord that Jesus carried.

There have been times when people have met me and "felt" the presence of God, which they later told me brought them to a place of repentance. This happened often in the ministry of the great evangelist Charles Finney. Writing about his own conversion (published in the tract Words of Life in 1921), he gave the following amazing account:

"I was powerfully converted on the morning of the 10th of October, 1821. In the evening of the same day I received overwhelming baptisms of the Holy Ghost, that went through me, as it seemed to me, body and soul. I immediately found myself endued with such power from on high that a few words dropped here and there to individuals were the means of their immediate conversion. My words seemed to fasten like barbed arrows in the souls of men. They cut like a sword. They broke the heart like a hammer. Multitudes can attest to this..."

Finney goes on to talk about his commitment to seeking the Lord to remain in the anointing:

"Sometimes I would find myself, in a great measure, empty of this power. I would go and visit, and find that I made no saving impression. I would exhort and pray, with the same result. I would then set apart a day for private fasting and prayer, fearing that this power had departed from me, and would inquire anxiously after the reason of this apparent emptiness. After humbling myself, and crying out for help, the power would return upon me with all its freshness. This has been the experience of my life."

Finney also speaks about how the "spiritual atmosphere" of a place can be changed by the manifest presence of God:

"Many times great numbers of persons in a community will be clothed with this power when the very atmosphere of the whole place seems to be charged with the life of God. Strangers coming into it, and passing through the place will be instantly smitten with conviction of sin and in many instances converted to Christ.

When Christians humble themselves and consecrate their all afresh to Christ, and ask for this power, they will often receive such a baptism that they will be instrumental in converting more souls in one day than in all their lifetime before. While Christians remain humble enough to retain this power, the work of conversion will go on, till whole communities and regions of country are converted to Christ."

Let us cooperate with the Holy Spirit to the extent that He can make us carriers of the presence of God, spreading the reverential fear of the Lord wherever we go and bringing the atmosphere of heaven.

Chapter 7

Communion With The Spirit

"What a joy to think that the same Spirit who was in Jesus during his days on earth is in me, and that He who Saint Basil called his inseparable companion is now also my inseparable companion, the sweet guest of my soul!"
– Raniero Cantalamessa
(from *Sober Intoxication of the Spirit: Filled with the Fullness of God*)

I love Paul's benediction in Corinthians 2, where he uses the intriguing phrase, "and the fellowship of the Holy Spirit be with you all" (2 Corinthians 13:14). The word for fellowship – koinónia – carries a sense of intimate partnership in which there is a joint sharing and contribution.

I like that. It describes who the Holy Spirit is to me. He has invited me into a partnership where He gets to share Himself with me and I share myself with Him. The Holy Spirit does not seek to possess me or control me. Rather, he seeks to fellowship with me in order to unlock all that Jesus is in me.

The point of the Holy Spirit coming upon us is, to use an Old Testament word, to "tabernacle" with us. The Tabernacle was the Tent of Meeting that contained God's manifest presence in the Holy of Holies. To "tabernacle" means to rest or abide with. The Holy Spirit wants to move in and live with us. In order for that to happen, we need to make Him welcome – because He's not going to barge in.

The Apostle John, who often employed Old Testament imagery to explain new revelation, speaks about the Holy Spirit as a dove coming to rest on Jesus. The image carries overtures of the Noah story, when the dove sought a place to rest and make its home. In Jesus, the Spirit found a "home" where He could abide. That same Person also wants to make His home with us.

When I was courting my wife, Katia, we were in a long distance relationship. I loved planning for her visits. I think of myself as a budding chef, so I enjoyed creating lovely meals for her and creating a romantic ambience. It was all part of my plan to woo her! I wanted to create just the right atmosphere and experience for her visit.

I think much of the Church treats the Holy Spirit this way. We are delighted to do the things necessary for an enjoyable visit, which is great, but He wants to do much more than just visit!

I was in for a rude awakening when Katia and I eventually married. Whilst I loved Katia suddenly sharing my space, I quickly realised that some rearrangement was going to be necessary. Furniture was moved around and added. Artwork that I personally loved was removed. Some things that were precious to me or to Katia now needed to somehow coexist. In short, habitation is very different to visitation!

For the Church to engage seriously with the Holy Spirit, both at a personal and corporate level, we have to move beyond "being open" to the Spirit and allow Him to move in. We have to build around Him, not invite Him to rubber stamp our agendas. We have to give Him the right to move (in some cases remove) the furniture, arrange it how He wants, and make Himself comfortable. Arguments about the style and content of our meetings become completely redundant when we tailor proceedings to accommodate the Holy Spirit. He is the one who can touch Christians and non-Christians alike, regardless of what is happening, when we have created an atmosphere in which He is free to move as He wills.

We are called to partner with Him in relationship. How does this work? Part of it has to be our conviction that he is a Person. In his commentary on Paul's teaching, Gordon Fee writes, "Whatever else is in Paul's thinking and experience, the Holy Spirit is not some kind of it, an impersonal force that comes from God. The Spirit is fully personal, indeed, in the language of a later time, 'God very God'" (from The Spirit and The People of God).

I may have laboured this point already, but we should relate to the Holy Spirit's personhood in the same way we relate to the Father's and Son's personhood. We shouldn't be afraid of praying to or chatting with the Holy Spirit. The Holy Spirit is God as much as the Father and Jesus are, and that makes Him deserved of our worship. He doesn't keep that worship to Himself, He reflects it onto the rest of the Trinity, because that's how He operates, but we don't need to get hung up on it. John 16 tells us that the Holy Spirit brings glory to Jesus by taking what belongs to Jesus and revealing it to us!

Designed to sense His presence

We have been designed to recognise the presence of the Spirit. In the beginning, we read that God walked in the garden in "the cool of the day" (Genesis 3:8) and Adam and Eve recognised His presence. The word translated "cool" – ruach – can also be translated "breeze" or "spirit". The same word is used in Genesis 1:2 to describe the Spirit of the Lord hovering over creation. What an incredible picture: the breeze of God's Spirit blowing gently through His garden. Adam sensed, and was surrounded by, the presence of God.

Of course, I believe in the omnipresence of God, yet we read that Adam and Eve hid from God's presence. We cannot hide from God's presence in a literal sense, but Adam and Eve "hid" from God because they knew something had changed in them and they were ashamed. Recognising God's presence suddenly brought guilt instead of joy.

In Luke 5:17 we read Luke's comments that as Jesus was teaching, "the power of the Lord was with him to heal". We know from Church history that Dr Luke was a physician. He was a natural choice to write both a Gospel and the book of Acts' orderly account of the formation and activity of the early Church. What interests me, however, is that this clearly learned man immediately recognised the presence of the Holy Spirit. He was able to observe and deduce that the presence of the Lord was near and available to heal.

I remember once praying in my lounge when presence of the Holy Spirit filled the room in a tangible way. I was completely overwhelmed by it. A few moments later my doorbell rang and it was one of my friends. I didn't mention that I'd been praying, but as soon as my friend stepped into the lounge he said, "Whoa! What's been happening in here? I can feel a whole lot of power in this room." People who are tuned in, immediately discern the Spirit's presence.

Being naturally supernatural

As the Church has grown in the West, we have moved ever further away from the Hebraic understanding of the world we live in. The early Church had a true biblical understanding of the holistic nature of the world – something that was naturally part of the Jewish mind set. In Jewish thinking, there is no distinction between the physical and spiritual aspects of life; so sacred and secular – everything belongs to God. In the West, however, we have separated the physical world from the spiritual, instead of treating the world as an integrated whole.

In his book The Pattern of New Testament Truth, George Eldon Ladd writes, "There is no antithesis between physical and spiritual life, between the outer and the inner dimensions in man, between the lower and higher realms. Life is viewed in its wholeness as the full enjoyment of all of God's gifts."

Many Christians find it difficult to accept that the Holy Spirit can speak and act using our natural faculties. They have inadvertently adopted the view that anything to do with our temporal bodies – the flesh, from which our redeemed bodies long to escape – is evil and cannot be trusted. But such a view is Gnosticism and a gross error. Our carnal nature is not the same as our physical flesh. Our bodies are so important to

God that one day they will be glorified. Our carnal natures, however, are dead and buried with Christ and can no longer exercise any hold over us.

Jesus redeems us spirit, soul and body, so we should expect the Holy Spirit to engage with us as total human beings, He is not just interested in the spiritual aspect of us. What does this mean in practice?

If we understand that the environment we live in has both a physical and spiritual aspect to it, we will live differently, with a heightened sense of awareness. The majority of people's focus is on the physical aspect of the world – what they can interact with using their normal senses. They can live in ignorance of the spiritual dimension of life – so much so, that any "spiritual" experiences they may have, they want to ignore or explain away. This is what happened in John 12 when people heard the voice of God speaking and explained it away, saying that they must have heard thunder. Others try to rationalise any supernatural experience in order to make it fit their personal beliefs. As someone has said, if all you have is a hammer, then everything looks like a nail!

If we are open to Him, however, the Holy Spirit will interact with us on a physical level as well as a spiritual level. Often when I minister, I feel a breeze on my face. The first time this happened I thought I must be standing near to an air conditioning unit. When it began to happen more often, I realised it was the Holy Spirit announcing His presence. It is often an invitation to me to tune into His will for a particular meeting or situation. The Holy Spirit loves to "inconvenience" us with His presence – to lead us in a different direction to the one in which we thought we were going. As we learn to trust Him and respond to these leadings, our sensitivity to Him deepens.

Sometimes God's presence will be accompanied by a sweet aroma or sweet taste in the mouth. Once, at a conference in Horsham, UK, many in the audience had their ears opened to the sounds of heaven. They heard musical instruments "joining in" with us as we sang and worshipped *a capella*.

There are times when I have had a strange taste in my mouth prior to receiving a word of knowledge. In a small prophetic meeting I was doing, I tasted the flavour of apple in my mouth and felt the Holy Spirit say that someone was allergic to apples. I had never heard such a word before, let alone thought that anyone might be allergic to apples. Added to that, the chances of somebody like that being present in a small gathering greatly increased the odds of getting it wrong! However, I brought the word and was able to get a young man's attention through it. The bit about the apple was just a precursor to what God really wanted to say to Him, and without grabbing his attention, he may have dismissed it.

In another meeting sparkling lights and flashes of lights could be seen as the Holy spirit manifested Himself. He does all these thing for various reasons and very spontaneously. I can't explain why, except to say that I think He knows that if He consistently showed up the same way, eventually we would want to make a formula out of our relationship with Him. His spontaneity helps us to remain dependent on Him.

It would be very easy to write off such supernatural happenings as coincidence and so miss the workings of the Spirit. The Bible tells us that Jacob managed to sleep through an encounter with God (Genesis 38). I believe that some of us do the same – people miss what the Holy Spirit is doing in our meetings because we are spiritually sleepy – not alert and mindful of what He might be doing. We need to practice the presence of God – to engage with Him, walk with Him, become familiar with His ways and His heart.

The Holy Spirit speaks to each one of us very differently. He treats us as the individuals we are. As we deepen our relationship with Him and recognise how He speaks to us, we become more familiar with the love language He uses to get our attention. The way He speaks to you will be different to how He speaks to me.

As we pursue a relationship with the Holy Spirit, He will also awaken our "spiritual senses". In other words, He can speak to us through dreams and visions – the ability to "see" in the Spirit. In John 1:48, the disciple Nathanael asks Jesus, "How do you know me?" Jesus responds by telling him He saw him sitting under a fig tree. Before He actually met Nathanael, the Holy Spirit showed him to Jesus. Jesus often "knew" what was in a person's heart by a word of knowledge, without anyone saying anything (John 2:24).

Retraining our mind

1 Corinthians 2:14 is a pivotal scripture in helping us to understand the naturally-supernatural dynamic.

"The natural person does not accept the things of the Spirit of God, for they are folly to him, and he is not able to understand them because they are spiritually discerned."

Paul often uses contrasts in his writing to underline his point: death to life, slavery to sonship, orphans to adoptees etc. He also contrasts the natural and the spiritual. I think we interpret the word "natural" to mean unspiritual, and assign more value to the spiritual, but this is not what Paul means. Here he is talking about the carnal nature versus the redeemed nature. Paul's argument is that only the spirit of a man truly knows what he is thinking, and now we have been given the Spirit of God, we are able to discern the mind of God. What an incredible privilege!

The problem we have with our minds is that we allow them to continue to be dominated by carnal thinking and this stems the flow of the Holy Spirit's revelation. In Matthew 16:23 Jesus rebuked Peter for trying to prevent Him from going to the cross: "Get behind me, Satan! You are a hindrance to me. For you are not setting your mind on the things of God, but on the things of man." Jesus put human wisdom on the same level as satanic inspiration.

So we have to get serious about renewing our minds. In Romans 12 Paul tells us to renew our minds in order to prove what is the acceptable and good and perfect will of God. I used to think that meant I needed to replace my bad thoughts with Scripture. In other words, memorise lots and lots of Bible verses in order to do better with my godly thinking. This is not what it means to renew our mind.

The word translated renew is the Greek word *anakainósis*. It is made up from *ana*, meaning "up" or "again" (literally, to think again) and *kainos*, which means "new in quality and form". Kainos is the world used when Paul writes that we are a "new creation". Paul is not saying that we are a better version of our old self, he is saying we are of a completely new and different quality. Our species of person has not been seen before and we carry the DNA of Jesus!

This means the renewing of our mind has to be done by "thinking again through the lens of our new creation". We have to think as those who have heaven in their DNA; those who realise that the impossible has become possible. This kind of mind is able to receive the things of the Spirit.

Our minds work in cooperation with our spirit to communicate with the Holy Spirit. In other words, if we want more interaction with the Holy Spirit, then we need to renew our minds such that His thoughts become ours. How do we do this? By spending time in His presence, being filled with Him! As a child of God, your privilege is the joy of having an intimate relationship with the Holy Spirit as He reveals the mind of God to you. You get to think like He does! Allow Him to speak to you through little thoughts and impressions. For more on how to hear His voice read my book, *Gaining Heaven's Perspective.*

Worship is the primary love language of the Holy Spirit. Philippians 3:3 says, "For we are the circumcision, who worship by the Spirit of God and glory in Christ Jesus and put no confidence in the flesh." Worship unlocks the presence of God. John 4:23-24 says, "But the hour is coming, and is now here, when the true worshipers will worship the Father in spirit and truth, for the Father is seeking such people to worship him. God is spirit, and those who worship him must worship in spirit and truth."

Where there is worship from the heart, the Holy Spirit seems to show up. It is in the context of worship that we will most easily discover and heart the voice of the Spirit. Worship creates an atmosphere in which the Holy Spirit loves to be!

Chapter 8

Tongues: Untapped Resource

"I thank God that I speak in tongues more than all of you."
(1 Corinthian 14:18)

I have been praying in tongues since I was three years old. I have found it to be an invaluable source of strength and joy and it has meant I have been privileged to drink deep of an intimate fellowship with and worship of Jesus. The Bible tells us that "praying in the Spirit" as it is otherwise known, edifies and builds us up. I have experienced this many times over. I have felt the inward strengthening presence of Jesus as I have worshipped Him using my personal heavenly language. Praying in the Spirit has been the key to resourcing all aspects of ministry and indeed my life.

In chapter 4 I quoted Terry Virgo from his book, The Spirit-Filled Church, as he recounted being baptised in the Holy Spirit. Regarding speaking in tongues he says, "I found myself not only speaking freely in tongues, but also calling out to

God in the most loving and intimate terms I could imagine." The gift of tongues was truly transformative in his life.

Speaking or praying in tongues has long been a contentious issue in the Church and over the years numbers of reformed pastors have taken a stand against it. I see this trend beginning to change, however, as many pastors and Bible scholars have revised their understanding of the Scriptures and embraced a "continuationist" view of the activity and gifts of the Holy Spirit.

Whatever your viewpoint, it has always intrigued me that Paul wrote more about the gift of tongues than any other gift. He also pointed out that he personally spoke in tongues more than any other person in the church at Corinth. Paul emphasised the use of the gift as appropriate both personally and corporately, in a local church setting. Despite all this, most Bible teachers, pastors and church members shy away from praying in tongues as a normal expression of their personal devotional and gathered church life.

Even more strongly than this, some pastors are going against the biblical imperative to "not forbid speaking in tongues" (1 Corinthians 14:39) and are trying to shut down the gift of tongues, either because they don't understand it or are fearful of it. Yet, the Church we see described early in Acts, and later on in the ministry of Paul, is full of power and robustly faces the challenges of sin and persecution in a way I do not see the contemporary Church doing. I wonder if there is a connection?

Why speak in tongues?
What's the big deal you might ask? What if I don't speak in

tongues? Why do I need to? Firstly, praying in tongues is not for God's benefit – it is His gift, specially designed for our benefit. Speaking in tongues helps our hearts articulate their deepest longings and desires through worship and adoration.

Tongues is a heavenly language which the Holy Spirit uses to empower us to pray when we have no idea what to pray:

"Likewise the Spirit helps us in our weakness. For we do not know what to pray for as we ought, but the Spirit himself intercedes for us with groanings too deep for words." (Romans 8:26)

The heavenly language of tongues connects us with heaven's reality like nothing else! Through it we are able to release faith.

Luke, writing in Acts, connects speaking in tongues to the declaration of God's glory (Acts 2:11) and Paul echoes this thought, speaking of the spread of the gospel (Acts 10:45-46). Here we see the first of the wider implications of speaking in tongues. It has an impact on others, drawing their attention to God.

Secondly, it has an impact on the gathered Church. The Holy Spirit is the conduit by which God's kingdom is released on the earth and when we pray in tongues we are cooperating with Him to see that future reality break in. The Wonderful Counsellor strengthens us to press in and take hold of the victory that is already secured for us.

Being built up

I love what Smith Wigglesworth had to say about the edifying impact of speaking in tongues in his own life:

"I want you to see that he who speaks in an unknown tongue

edifies himself or builds himself up. We must be edified before we can edify the church. I cannot estimate what I, personally, owe to the Holy Ghost's method of spiritual edification. I am here before you as one of the biggest conundrums in the world. There never was a weaker man on the platform. Language? None. Inability – full of it. All natural things in my life point exactly opposite to my being able to stand on the platform and preach the gospel.

The secret is that the Holy Ghost came and brought this wonderful edification of the Spirit. I had been reading this Word continually, as well as I could, but the Holy Ghost came and took hold of it, for the Holy Ghost is the breath of it, and He illuminated it to me. And He gives me language that I cannot speak fast enough; it comes too fast; and it is there because God has given it. When the Comforter is come He shall teach you ALL things; and He has given me this supernatural means of speaking in an unknown tongue to edify myself, so that, after being edified, I can edify the church." (see http://www.smithwigglesworth.com/sermons/eif18.htm for the full transcript of Wigglesworth's sermon)

I have found that stirring myself by praying in the Spirit creates in me an expectation of the Holy Spirit to move through me. I regularly use the gift of tongues to build myself up before ministering in a church meeting and whenever I do, I visibly see the results. I don't limit this to church meetings, however. I will pray when I drive my car, on the train (under my breath!), and as I go about my daily chores. All of this prepares me for God to use me to extend His kingdom whenever the opportunity arises to step out in faith.

Again I quote Smith Wigglesworth:

"It is a wonderful thing to pray in the Spirit and to sing in the Spirit, praying in tongues and singing in tongues as the Spirit of God gives you utterance. I never get out of bed in the morning without having communion with God in the Spirit. It is the most wonderful thing on earth. It is most lovely to be in the Spirit when you are dressing and you come out to the world and the world has no effect on you. You begin the day like that and you will be conscious of the guidance of the Spirit right through the day."

Through praying in tongues God invites us to seek out the hidden mysteries of His will and reveals them to us by His Spirit.

"For one who speaks in a tongue speaks not to men but to God; for no one understands him, but he utters mysteries in the Spirit." (1 Corinthians 14:2)

When we pray in tongues it enables the Holy Spirit to share the deep things of God with us. When we speak in tongues, we don't understand the words being spoken with our minds, yet the Holy Spirit is able to communicate with our Spirit, imparting truth and revelation.

I will often pray in tongues as I'm preparing sermons or just studying Scripture. As I do, the Holy Spirit seems to unlock more revelation to me. I spend time reading and re-reading verses whilst continuing to pray in tongues, so that while my mind is busy reading, my spirit is engaged with the praying! This seems to trigger thoughts that lead to a deeper understanding of the truth I'm reading.

Another aspect of the "mysteries" that are unlocked in us is learning to pray according to the will of the Holy Spirit. "...we do not know what to pray for ... but the Spirit himself intercedes for us...". There are times when God directs us to "do battle" in tongues regarding issues about which we have no clue. In an article on his website, Sam Storms writes that "Praying in tongues may also be an effective instrument in spiritual warfare ... Paul describes tongues in 1 Corinthians 14:16 as praying or blessing 'in (the) spirit' (en pneumati). In Ephesians 6:18 he encourages us to pray "in (the) spirit" (en pneumati), using the same terminology. The exhortation in this passage addressing our struggle with principalities and powers, although not limited to praying in tongues, most likely includes it."

In other words, praying in tongues can help us overcome fear and the Holy Spirit can use these "supercharged" prayers to protect us in difficult or dangerous circumstances. A few years ago, whilst an Elder at The Bay Community Church, Cape Town, some friends and I went for dinner after the Sunday night meeting. We did this regularly and on this particular night, a group of eight of us entered the restaurant and occupied the biggest table. Suddenly, two armed men burst in and began to rob and "rustle" up the customers. As we realised what was happening I told my friends to all pray in tongues. The armed robbers walked around our table three times before realising that we were there. We seemed to be invisible to them, despite being the biggest table in the restaurant. By the time they realised we were there, they became aware that the police were on the way and fled the restaurant. Incredibly, we were the only people not to be robbed that night. In such a situation, we had no idea what to pray, but as we prayed in tongues we prayed according to the Spirit and we experienced God's protection on us.

Can everyone speak in tongues?

You might be reading this thinking, "I want this gift, but is it really for all Christians? Will God give it to me?"

In 1 Corinthians 12:28-30 Paul seems to imply that not every believer has to speak in tongues. But it is equally clear in Scripture that most accounts of the filling of the Holy Spirit are accompanied by speaking in tongues, joy or prophecy. In his Alpha course book, Questions of Life, Nicky Gumbel points out, "Not every Christian speaks in tongues. Yet Paul says: 'I would like every one of you to speak in tongues,' suggesting that it is not only for a special class of Christian. It is open to all Christians."

It is my personal belief that one does not have to speak in tongues as a sign of baptism in the Spirit. It is my conviction, however, that anyone can receive this free gift and often it is simply unhelpful models, teaching and expectations that stop us from receiving this wonderful prayer language. Some common obstacles to receiving this gift are:

- An unclear understanding of the Father heart of God towards us and His strong desire to give us gifts
- Feeling underserving or disqualified
- Anxiety that, if prayed for, one might not receive it
- Theological misunderstanding
- Fear of not being in control of ourselves

These are typical examples, but irrespective of this, God can and will break in! All He is looking for is a thirsty heart. Over the years I have prayed for thousands of people to be baptised in the Spirit and to have the ability to speak in tongues (the majority of whom began speaking in tongues instantly after receiving clear teaching).

For many, the key was realising that the gift of tongues is not inspired by our mind. In fact, when we exercise the gift of tongues the Bible says that our mind is unfruitful (1 Corinthians 14:13). It is in fact a biblical response to say, "This does not make any sense to my mind!"

If you have not received the gift of tongues and would like to do so, why not turn to Appendix 1 now. Here you will find how to enter into this wonderful experience today. Be expectant. Remember that God loves to give you good gifts.

"If you then, who are evil, know how to give good gifts to your children, how much more will the heavenly Father give the Holy Spirit to those who ask him!" (Luke 11:13)

Chapter 9

Joy: Signature of the Spirit

"And the disciples were filled with joy and with the Holy
Spirit."
(Acts 13:52)

Wherever the Holy Spirit is there is joy! Scripture tells us that
the kingdom of God is "living a life of goodness and peace
and joy in the Holy Spirit" (Romans 14:17). Joy is a hallmark
of those who have been filled with the Holy Spirit. Yet, it is
the least evident expression of many local churches, let alone
individual Christians. Unfortunately, I see many in the Church
who seem to live joyless, powerless lives. Why powerless?
Because in the Bible joy and strength are inextricably linked. It
is the joy of the Lord that provides strength (Nehemiah 8:10).

Katia and I had an interesting time in the run up to our
wedding day. There was the usual, enjoyable, build up that
involved choosing colour schemes, sending out invites and
most importantly (for me) choosing the food and wine. My

parents had flown over from South Africa to attend the wedding and all was set for the celebration of a lifetime. Little did we know how challenging our day would prove to be.

A few weeks prior to our wedding I'd had a dream in which I saw my mother die on our wedding day. I prayed about this and trusted God with it. It wasn't until my mom suddenly fell ill a few days before the wedding that I realised how serious this dream was.

We were plunged into a time of uncertainty. Mom was admitted to hospital and tests were run. Daily we waited for reports from her doctors and, at every turn, she simply got worse. More difficult than that was the fact that they couldn't seem to get to the bottom of what was wrong with her. Day after day went by and she became ever more dangerously sick.

Soon the day before the wedding arrived. Final preparations were being made when I received a call from the hospital. The doctors had put Mom into an induced coma and were encouraging me to come and say my goodbyes. There did not seem to be any hope of her recovering. I remember weeping and thinking this cannot be so. I reluctantly phoned my bride-to-be and told her the news that we might not get married in the morning. What was meant to be a joyous celebration was fast becoming an occasion for mourning.

Both our families were amazing in the support they gave us My dad and my sister so loved me in the midst of having to process their own grief and the prospect of not seeing my mom at the wedding. As I went to bed that night, or should I say tried to go to bed, I had to talk this over with God. I was trying to figure out what was going on. I prayed in tongues for a long time, waiting and listening. As I began to breakthrough in prayer I realised I had to make a decision in my heart: was God good or not?

This is fundamental to how we approach life. The Holy Spirit loves to reveal Jesus to us. He unlocks the mind of God to us (1 Corinthians 2:9-12). He helps us understand what God is like and one of the earliest revelations of God is that He is good. He cannot be anything other than good. When His goodness is the foundation of your life, joy is the result and this comes to us by the Spirit.

That night, as I sat on my bed praying, I had to resolve in my mind to accept the fact that God was still good, despite my circumstances. God is not the author of evil (James 1:13). He is not the author of suffering, but He allows suffering in our lives sometimes to produce endurance and character (Romans 5:3-5). Despite this, His goodness remains constant (Psalm 107:1).

As I resolved to trust in the goodness of God, no matter what, the Holy Spirit began to sustain me. I felt that God wanted us to press ahead with the wedding. My Mom remained in a coma and I prayed that God would somehow intervene.

The next day at our wedding there was a deep sense of loss that my precious mother was not there and yet, our wedding was marked by an outpouring of Holy Spirit joy. During the ceremony itself, the presence of God descended thickly and broke into the proceedings. I literally had to hold Katia up as we made our vows. Joy was in the house!

One person commented that they had never felt the presence of the Holy Spirit at a wedding like they did on that day. Joy in the Holy Spirit strengthened us. I am happy to say that not only did we make it through the day, but my mother was raised up from her death bed and is still continuing in ministry alongside my father. We were put to the test, but God is incredibly good!

Living in joy

In life, all kinds of situations and circumstances will try to assault our joy and peace. How we react to these things is crucial. Do we fall into despair? React with frustration and anger? Or do we run into the fortress of the Lord and meditate in His temple (Psalm 27). Learning to live in joy by the Spirit is the greatest privilege. Joy is key to our understanding of spiritual warfare. The Bible says that God laughs at His enemies (Psalm 2:4). When we live in joy, aware of our position in Christ, we can approach difficulties and spiritual attack from a place of rest, secure in God's presence.

The Bible tells us that Jesus is seated at the right hand of the father (Mark 16:19). This is picture language, because in priestly terms, sitting indicates that the priest's work is completed (Hebrews 10:11-14). Jesus is our High Priest who has accomplished everything on our behalf. This means that when the battle comes to us and we must engage in spiritual warfare, we do so not to fight for victory – we fight from victory. Jesus has already won. We need to learn to laugh, be joyful and simply celebrate what is already ours, regardless of the fact that everything seems to be against us.

Joy has great purpose in it. The Bible says that it was for the joy that was set before Him that Jesus endured the cross (Hebrews 12:2). His joy was what set Jesus apart from other prophets. He was anointed with gladness above His companions! (Hebrews 1:9) The word translated "gladness" in this verse conveys the idea of the emotion of happiness gushing forth, welling up with joy and allowing it to spill out everywhere.

Jesus was happy because despite the suffering He had to endure, He knew that joy would be the result. Wonderfully, you and I are His joy! Joy does not deny suffering, rather it helps us to walk through it.

Joy is the culture of the kingdom. I have found that releasing joy results in a greater display of kingdom activity. Joy seems to open up healing and the flow of the Spirit's power more directly. I have often wondered if it has something to do with that scripture which says "a joyful heart is good medicine" (Proverbs 17:22). Once people get filled with joy, it takes their eyes off their sickness and somehow releases healing. The most memorable healing meetings I've been a part of have happened as joy has broken out. Wherever we see the kingdom of God break out, joy and freedom result.

There are those who have used so called "maturity" as an excuse for a lack of joy, but the Bible is clear that maturity and joy are not mutually exclusive. I like the C. S. Lewis quote from his book Letters to Malcolm: Chiefly on Prayer, that says, "Joy is the serious business of heaven."

Joy is indeed a serious matter! It's why Jesus went to the Father. It's part of our adoption. Jesus instructs us to "Ask, and you will receive, that your joy may be full" (John 16:24). The Passion translation of this verse says "that your joy will have no limits". This is Jesus speaking about the coming of the Holy Spirit when He leaves His disciples. Although He was returning to His Father, He was about to release limitless joy through the Holy Spirit.

I have often witnessed great outpourings of joy and laughter in meetings around the world. It is the displays of laughter, hilarity and "drunkenness" which are particularly offensive to the religious mind – yet such things were common in the New Testament Church and they have characterised moves of God throughout history. People filled to overflowing with joy is a natural manifestation of the moving of God's Spirit.

I recall one gentleman getting very upset and rebuking me for being preoccupied with emotionalism. His view was that uncontained joy was simply too fleshly and emotional. My response to him was that joy is not an emotion, but a fruit of the Spirit (Galatians 5:22) and it should be seen in the life of the believer.

Katia often teaches on this and makes the point that joy is a fundamental expression of the Christian life. It is why Jesus constantly used the word "blessed" to describe the state of the believer. It means being ecstatically happy. Joy has to be visible – everyone can sense and see when we are joyful; it's impossible to hide it. I fear that many in the Church have been baptised in lemon juice and as a result, tried to redefine joy!

Yet, joy is like the doorway to God's kingdom – the entry point, the defining characteristic. Joy is what Jesus calls us to. True joy in the Holy Spirit is much bigger, deeper and wider than mere happiness. We try to reduce it to a mere emotion, but actually the Bible describes joy as inexpressible and full of glory (1 Peter 1:8).

Our Father desires us to be filled with joy. In Deuteronomy 28:47 the people of God were rebuked for offering Him sacrifices without joy. I can only imagine what it is like to have someone you love with all your heart serve you out of a sense of duty instead of joy. If my wife only expressed service to me as an act of duty, I'd be devastated! We serve each other because of our love and joy of being together.

I come back to the point I made at the beginning of this chapter. Too many of us live lives that are governed by external circumstances. We are happy when things are going well and unhappy when they are not. Joy becomes transient when we live like this. Whether we are joyful will depend on our circumstances.

We need to re-orientate our minds and tune into heaven's perspective of our situation, allowing the Holy Spirit to guide the way we approach life. Instead of floundering in our circumstances, we need to learn to agree with God's assessment of our situation and lean on His truth. Instead of living under our circumstances, we need to live in the superior reality of God's kingdom, despite what might be going on.

The Bible is strong on joy. It commands us to be joyful. How do we do this? We can practice joy. Read the Psalms as the perfect example of remaining committed to joy, regardless of external circumstances. Time and time again the Psalmist falls back on the constancy of the goodness of God. Time and again, the writer determines to express joy, regardless. Worship is a key to joy. Most of the Psalms instruct us to do something in our worship: sing, lift up your hands, dance, be still. We are told to "shout for joy" (Psalm 33:1), praise God with joyful lips (Psalm 63:5) or to "make a joyful noise" (Psalm 95:1). Joy is a lifestyle choice. We can practice joy.

When joy becomes our habitual response, we can laugh

even in the midst of suffering. I constantly ask the Holy Spirit to fill me with His joy — the mark of His presence. Psalm 16:11 says, "You make known to me the path of life; in your presence is fullness of joy…" Staggering and wonderful. This verse hit me between the eyes when I read it. It means that our destiny in life is connected to enjoying God's presence. The path He has for your life is found in His presence, filled with joy!

Jesus invites us into joy as a natural overflow of our relationship with Him and this comes by the Spirit. When Jesus spoke of the outpouring of the Spirit He said, "No one will take your joy from you!" (John 16:22). This life of joy is not just for heaven, but for now!

Chapter 10

A Future People

"A voice cries: In the wilderness prepare the way of the
LORD; make straight in the desert a highway for our God."
(Isaiah 40:3)

"The Christian life is expressed in an eschatological tension.
We live in view of two ages working together."
– Derek Morphew
(Breakthrough: Discovering the Kingdom)

As believers we are living in two worlds. We are here on earth,
but the Bible tells us to focus on the realities of heaven:

"Since you have been raised to new life with Christ, set
your sights on the realities of heaven, where Christ sits in the
place of honour at God's right hand." (Colossians 3:1 NLT)

While most people consider the world around them to be
"reality", in fact a greater reality exists beyond that which is
seen and felt. The Apostle Paul spoke a lot about this "tension"

that we live in – a tension that, when properly understood, is gloriously liberating and empowering. We are called to fix our eyes on that which is unseen (2 Corinthians 4:18). This is the essence of faith. Our faith is not rooted in the transient nature of the world, but in the eternal reality of the realm of the Living God.

Let's explore this though some more. I want to help you to see that the Holy Spirit desires to empower you to live in kingdom tension – His power irresistibly bubbling out of you to bring heaven on earth.

Trusting in the unseen

In the model prayer Jesus used to teach His disciples to pray, He said, "Father, let your will be done on earth as it is in heaven." As modern day disciples of Jesus, ours is the privilege on knowing that life on earth is impacted as heaven invades earth through us. Right here is the "tension" Paul speaks of: heaven has come to earth and is available now, yet we still live in the reality of a fallen world. Even though the kingdom of God has come and is coming, we still see so many areas that need kingdom breakthrough.

Let me share a personal example. I have had the privilege of praying for many hundreds of people with various sicknesses or diseases. Two areas in which I have seen the Lord consistently heal people are back problems and allergies. The kingdom of God has broken through and many have been healed instantaneously. God is so good! Yet, the things that I personally suffer most with are back problems and allergies!

I can't explain why this is the case. I don't understand it, but I continue to believe in faith that one day God will heal me of both conditions. One thing that is not an option is for me to question God's goodness because of this issue. If I allow offence to creep in against the character of God, then I am left faithless and powerless. Do I know it is the will of God to heal? Yes I do. Do I know that my God is good? Yes I do. This is what fuels my faith, believing that God will heal me in His time. Parallel to this is my understanding that I am part of an ever-increasing kingdom, so my expectation is that sooner, rather than later, I will be healed. This is the tension of the "now and not yet" of God's kingdom.

In the past, I believe many theologians have produced teaching that has sought to "explain" their lack of experience of the things of the Spirit, without responsibly teaching believers to have an expectation of God's kingdom breaking in. I think this has given birth to a doctrine and practice that causes Christians to rely more on what is seen than unseen, relying more on the faculty of intellect than faith in the reality of heaven. One consequence of this is that we now have to battle to convince people that our God is a healing God. Wider than this, we have to help people understand that supernatural manifestations are signs that the kingdom of God is near, and that they are not the work of the enemy!

A cerebral, "show me proof, then I'll believe" approach to the Christian life is not what the Bible teaches. Our lives should mirror the reality of the coming kingdom and that should affect our daily life. Repeatedly, Jesus teaches that we should have an impact on society, cleared marked by how we live. We read in Acts 1:3 that Jesus, post-resurrection, appeared to His disciples numerous times over a period of 40 days and spoke constantly about the impact of the kingdom of God.

The call of the people of the future

All that the kingdom releases and reveals is found in the Holy Spirit. He is the guarantee of our inheritance in the kingdom (Ephesians 1:14). We are supposed to be living in the reality of this other world, this kingdom which cannot be shaken here and now! (Hebrews 12:28) We are to be a people of the future!

John the Baptist began his career by preparing the way for the inauguration of this future kingdom (Luke 3). His work was the prelude to Jesus' work of making the kingdom of heaven accessible. John's revolutionary message, "Repent, for the kingdom of God is at hand" (Matthew 3:2) called people to change the way they thought about the kingdom. For the first time someone was saying that the kingdom of God was in arm's reach; closer than anyone could imagine.

John was an unusual and unlikely looking forerunner of Jesus. He lived out in the wilderness in less than glamorous surroundings. His diet was that of basic survival food! He was radical, uncompromising and wild looking. Most of us would probably have felt uncomfortable being around John! Yet, he was filled with the Holy Spirit from his mother's womb and he lived full of divine expectation. He grew up with a future hope inside him. He knew that something big was about to hit planet earth.

John was the last and the greatest of all the Old Testament prophets, standing at the transition point between old and new covenant. Yet, Jesus says that the least of us believers is "greater" than John (Matthew 11:11). Why did He say this? I believe it is because we not only get to declare this future kingdom to others, like John, but we also get to share in the same ministry of Jesus – to demonstrate that the future is here and now. What a high calling.

What heaven on earth looks like

This is the call of a people of the future. We live in a demonstration of the design, purpose and joy of heaven here on earth. This has massive implications for how we build our lives, our churches and how we interact with a lost and dying world.

For example, how we worship should be affected by our revelation of heaven. The Bible tells us that every tribe, every tongue every people will worship God – a glorious display of His divine wisdom (Revelation 7:9-12). A multi-cultural, united body is what heaven looks like, therefore we need to reflect that future reality now. It means our worship should often include different rhythms, sounds and languages – not because we are trying to be inclusive or politically correct, but because that's what heaven looks like!

Another area that has to be affected is how we work with those who are poor and destitute. In heaven there is no need, no pain, no tears (Revelation 21:4). Our work amongst the poor, therefore, cannot simply be social action or benevolent aid, it must include a full outworking of the power of the kingdom. It must be much more than simply fulfilling a person's physical needs – it has to be about seeing the broken made whole and the poor lifted from the ash heap of life! (Psalm 113:7-9)

In fact, all areas of our Christian lives should be characterised by the Spirit's power, because that is what is happening in heaven. Christ is seated at the right hand of God (Mark 16:19) and we are seated with Christ in heavenly places (Ephesians 2:6). We need to build churches and communities that reflect the realities of heaven. We are called to be a city on a hill; a light that brings illumination and revelation to a lost and dying world! (Matthew 5:14)

Extra-ordinary believers

Malachi 3 is a key passage that speaks about a generation to come who will move in the power and spirit of Elijah, to turn the hearts of fathers to their sons, and sons to their fathers – in other, words a ministry of restoration and reconciliation that sees many prodigals come home. I believe that the generation the prophet spoke of is the Church.

The Church is called to hasten the day of the Lord (2 Peter 3:11-12) and has the freedom to move in power and to demonstrate the Father heart of God. The Church is becoming a company of people who move in signs and wonders as a radical demonstration of the kingdom. Many of these extra-ordinary believers will look like unlikely candidates in the eyes of the world, but will move in supernatural power. My belief and expectation is that as God's kingdom manifests itself on the earth in increasing measure we will see everyday, unremarkable believers moving in power, even praying and seeing the dead raised! Yet, power will not be the most important aspect of this company – rather it will be releasing the Father's heart. This will be the distinguishing difference between those who are genuine followers of Jesus and those who are peddling counterfeit spirituality. This future is found in the Holy Spirit. It is why Jesus said, "He will take what is mine and make it known to you" (John 16:14).

Culture shapers

One of the most intriguing aspects of the Holy Spirit's nature is His creativity. The following verses from Exodus 30:31-35 have always grabbed my attention. Look how the Holy Spirit expresses Himself:

"Then Moses said to the people of Israel, 'See, the LORD has called by name Bezalel the son of Uri, son of Hur, of the tribe of Judah; and he has filled him with the Spirit of God, with skill, with intelligence, with knowledge, and with all craftsmanship, to devise artistic designs, to work in gold and silver and bronze, in cutting stones for setting, and in carving wood, for work in every skilled craft. And he has inspired him to teach, both him and Oholiab the son of Ahisamach of the tribe of Dan. He has filled them with skill to do every sort of work done by an engraver or by a designer or by an embroiderer in blue and purple and scarlet yarns and fine twined linen, or by a weaver—by any sort of workman or skilled designer.'"

I find this stunning. The Holy Spirit is far from boring and predictable. He loves creativity, design and craftsmanship. The Spirit filled the craftsmen mentioned above and His creativity flowed through them. This is significant for us today, because we need to recapture an understanding of the opportunities we have as believers to shape culture, inspired by the creativity of God!

Think about writers of years gone by, such as C. S. Lewis, whose works still speak today. Lewis used gripping stories and allegories to demonstrate kingdom truths. Think of the amazing works of art which adorn many of our ancient cathedrals. We each need to play our part in using our creativity to shape culture and impact the world with expressions of God's kingdom.

Recently I met a young man who has used computer gaming videos on his YouTube channel to creatively communicate the gospel to others. He shares his testimony of how God healed him of severe food allergies and his videos have received well over 2 million hits. My friend Brad Klynsmith has written a number of songs which have been in the top ten in the music charts, and which have shaped the consciousness of a generation in South Africa, causing them to think about their spirituality.

More and more I am hearing stories of people beginning to have influence in the creative arena. The Holy Spirit loves to teach us to use our creativity and in doing so extend His kingdom powerfully.

We must think differently and reimagine what it means to be part of this kingdom. We have to engage with the Holy Spirit and cooperate with His agenda to release the kingdom of God on the earth. The key is remaining in close fellowship with Him:

"When the Spirit of truth comes, he will guide you into all the truth, for he will not speak on his own authority, but whatever he hears he will speak, and he will declare to you the things that are to come. He will glorify me, for he will take what is mine and declare it to you." (John 16:13-14)

Kingdom living means that our relationship with the Holy Spirit directs everything we do on earth. He is the power for the transformation of the world. He is the key to experiencing some future kingdom reality now.

Chapter 11

Impartation: Power To Act!

"For I long to see you, that I may impart to you some
spiritual gift to strengthen you."
(Romans 1:11)

The most significant changes that have produced powerful
fruit in my life have all come from times of impartation by the
Spirit. This word "impart" means to "offer by way of change;
offer so that a change of owner is produced or to give a share
of" (Strong's Greek 3330). Impartation happens when the
Holy Spirit uses a person to touch another person with His
power, and releases a particular spiritual gift.

I will never forget meeting Dr James Maloney – an
incredible gift to the body of Christ. James is full of integrity,
good character and moves in incredible creative miracles.
Along with these power manifestations, he also moves in
phenomenal accuracy when it comes to prophecy. Few
people I have seen operate in an anointing like this.

James and I were sharing speaking duties at a conference at my home church, The King's Arms, and we met for the first time at the opening meeting. Having been introduced, we were sitting together on the front row when James turned to me and said, "Son, today you will receive an impartation from me." We proceeded with the meeting and ministered alongside each other, after which James prayed a simple prayer of impartation. At that moment, I felt as though I had been kicked in the chest by a donkey and was floored by the power of God as the Holy Spirit came and overwhelmed me.

From that day onwards I began to notice a significant increase in creative miracles when I prayed for others, including a significant element of James' own ministry: he often prays for those who have had serious structural surgery involving metal plates. God heals those people and the metal literally dissolves away. As well as this, I noticed a sharpening of my prophetic gift, with an increased level of accuracy.

Another significant impartation happened when I met Shawn Bolz, an amazing apostolic leader from Los Angeles. Shawn moves in the gift of words of knowledge and often delivers incredibly accurate words and seems to interact powerfully with the angelic. I had the privilege of being in his meetings and sharing a conference with him in Dubai. After being around Shawn my own awareness of angelic assistance increased. This didn't come as a result of Shawn laying hands on me, but simply from me being in faith and earnestly desiring an increased anointing from the Lord.

You might say, Julian what is your point?

My point is this: in our cautiousness to engage with the supernatural, which arises from a fear of being deceived, we are missing out on a vital aspect of our empowerment – that of allowing gifted ministries to impart and release spiritual gifts in us.

From the Old Testament to the New, impartation is part of the fabric of the spiritual life. We see it in the lives of Moses (Numbers 11:25), Saul (1 Samuel 19:24), Peter and John (Acts), Paul (Romans 1:11) and Timothy (1 Timothy 4:14).

Many Christians underestimate the power of impartation or are afraid to make themselves vulnerable to an anointed servant of God. It's not uncommon. The people of Nazareth missed out on a powerful visitation in their city because they failed to recognise the anointing of Jesus (Matthew 13:57; Mark 6:4) and could not therefore receive anything from Him. Jesus rebuked their unbelief and connected it to a lack of honour.

Honour means to ascribe worth and value to something. When we don't honour ministries, then we are cutting off the possibility of receiving impartation. Lest you think that I am suggesting we place "specially anointed minister" on pedestals, this is not what I'm getting at.

Danny Silk, in his book A Culture of Honour, writes, "the principle of honour states that accurately acknowledging who people are will position us to give them what they deserve and to receive the gift of who they are in our lives." So honour is about recognising the grace that has been applied to another person's life; about valuing them for who they are. Ultimately, the Bible calls us to honour everyone, including those who are lost (1 Peter 2:17).

Parallel to a lack of honour, offence is perhaps the biggest barrier to receiving an impartation of the Holy Spirit. In the

Bible, both the widow from Nain and the military leader Naaman had to do things that were personally offensive to them in order to receive the breakthrough they desired. It called for humility and personal vulnerability. In Jesus' day, many people missed out on receiving from Him because He wasn't what they expected and His approach offended them. Often, the gifted ministries who carry an anointing and can help us to grow in the Spirit come in packages we don't expect.

This is the inconvenient thing about the Holy Spirit – He often uses people who don't fit our theological expectations to impart to us! Part of this must be because He simply invites us to make ourselves vulnerable to Him and part of it must be His insistence on using less than perfect vessels, so that only Jesus can get the glory.

Smith Wigglesworth was known for his brash, Yorkshire temperament. Kathryn Kuhlman often seemed eccentric. Lonnie Frisbee, who was involved in pioneering the Vineyard movement, was a hippie from the Jesus Movement.

My simple point is that we should honour people for who they are, not for who they are not. Recognising the grace that God has placed on someone is an important step towards partnering with the Holy Spirit and receiving what He has invested in them to bring about fruit in our lives. That's how impartation works. We may have had bad experiences in the past, but let's not throw out the baby with the bath water.

Stewarding the anointing

Sometimes people come to me, having recognised the gift of God at work, and want me to impart to them what God has invested in me. Of course, all gifting of the Holy Spirit comes by grace, not works, and I am always glad to pray for anyone. But how an impartation is stewarded is very important. Sometimes people are looking for a shortcut. They want to operate in spiritual power without going through the process of hard won victories and failures that form a part of the life of any servant of the gospel.

Just because we receive an impartation from a seasoned minister of the gospel, does not mean we will automatically begin to function in the same level of gifting and authority as them. How we steward what God gives us will determine the yield of fruitfulness.

Each time I have seen an increase of God's anointing in my life I have been through a prior season of growth and preparation. How we use what God has already given us is a determining factor in our spiritual growth. Fruitfulness flows from good stewarding of the gifts of the Holy Spirit. When we receive an impartation we have to activate it to move in it. When men and women who carry particular grace pray for me, I always look for an opportunity to step out and do what they do. Often this results in failure! But with obedience and persistence, I begin to see some breakthroughs.

God is pleased with and attracted to faith. We are often preoccupied with results. If we get good results we celebrate and vice versa. But God celebrates faith. Abraham didn't always do everything right, but he certainly stepped out in faith and God rewarded him for it. Faith takes risks. Sometimes the risk of stepping out after receiving an impartation is not met with success, but we should take heart and persist with an expectation of seeing the kingdom break out.

I have often gotten discouraged when I've given out words of knowledge and it appears I've got it wrong – particularly when I felt I had something very specific to share. Stepping out like that is daunting. Thankfully I am God's favourite (and so are you!) and my standing with Him is not determined by my success or failure in ministry. I don't have to "get it right" in order to be in His favour.

Prayer for impartation

Remember, we grow in the Holy Spirit when we allow others to impart to us the grace that they have received from the Lord. Ask the Holy Spirit to help you recognise this and don't be afraid to ask for it and receive it.

God has been so kind to me and I have been privileged to see Him do some amazing things. Whilst I have so much more to learn, experience and enjoy in God, I want to end this book by humbly praying for you to receive an impartation of greater intimacy, gifts and anointing of the Spirit. If you want to receive this, please agree with this prayer from my heart to yours:

"Dear Father, I thank you for this precious reader – a child you have created. I thank you too for all the things you have done in my life. I want to impart all the good things you have given me freely in your Holy Spirit. Thank you, Holy Spirit, for your constant friendship with me. Would you impart increased grace to this reader to walk in greater intimacy, gifts and the power that you give.

I pray that my best moment in the Spirit would be their starting point. Let my ceiling be their platform. I pray for an army of sons and daughters who know the wonderful

Counsellor and truth teller. Let them know and experience deep fellowship with you, Holy Spirit, and cause it to grow in an ever-increasing way. Thank you for them and bless them in Jesus' name. Amen."

Appendix
How Will I Know When I've Been Baptised in the Spirit?

Because we can sometimes get confused about the process, I offer in this Appendix a simple checklist for testing whether you have been baptised in the Holy Spirit. There is a prayer you can pray at the end to receive the fullness of the Holy Spirit.

A. You receive power
1. But you will receive power when the Holy Spirit comes upon you. (Acts 1:8)
2. The disciples, still hiding after the resurrection were transformed. They had new boldness, authority and faith.
3. Paul received power and was healed. (Acts 9:17-18)
4. Something visibly changed the Samaritans (Acts 8:17-18). This should be our experience also.

B. You receive joy (Acts 2:13-15)

C. You receive revelation

1. Jesus received confirmation of His identity from the Father. (Matthew 3:16-17)
2. The disciples understood Jesus' purpose and message more than they ever did while they were with him (Acts 2).

D. Tongues and Prophecy

1. These normally come with the baptism in the Spirit (Acts 2:4, Acts 10:46; 19:6). There is no mention of other gifts coming at this time.
2. Don't be afraid – nothing God does is contrary to His character.
3. Our present understanding is that one can be baptised in the Spirit and not speak to God in tongues. But if you are baptised in the Spirit you have the ability to speak to God in tongues and you should use the gift (Acts 2:4). Whether you choose to use it or not is your decision. *Note: Your experience won't necessarily be like that of others.*

Remember:

a) Don't compare your experience with testimonies you've heard.
b) The promise is that the Holy Spirit will come, not necessarily as a mighty wind, etc. Sometimes He comes like a dove, sometimes like Acts 2:13.

How To Receive The Baptism In The Holy Spirit (John 7:37-39)

**A. You must have a personal relationship with Jesus (v38).
The baptism in the Spirit is for believers (Acts 11:17).**

B. You must be thirsty (v37)
   1. You don't need to be perfect, or totally free.
   2. A thirsty person is aware of his need. Thirst is one of the strongest desires of the human body.
   3. Are you aware of your need for power and freedom?

C. You must come to Jesus (v37)
   1. Go to Jesus Himself, not to a leader in the church.
   2. Laying on of hands helps you receive from Jesus.

D. You must drink
   1. You don't need to plead, try to earn, or to wait. The reason the disciples had to wait was that Jesus was not yet glorified.
   2. Ask, expecting to receive (Luke 11:9-13). It is a sure promise of the Father (Acts 2.33-39). *Drink – don't be passive. This requires faith.*

E. Allow the river to flow
   1. When the Holy Spirit comes upon you, relax, thank God and receive.
   2. Then speak. Don't wait for it to happen. God gives you the ability, speak to Him and not those around you.
   3. Prophesy as you receive insight, revelation or burdens.

To help you receive, pray this prayer:

Father, I thank you for giving us your Spirit. Jesus you are the one who baptises me with the Holy Spirit. Please fill me now. I receive your free gift now by faith. And I also now receive the ability to speak in tongues. Amen.

Now simply take a deep breath and begin to speak whatever words form and flow from you. Your mind will protest and say this is weird (that's a biblical response!) Now begin to worship Jesus in your new language.

About the Author

Julian is from Cape Town, South Africa, and grew up in a pioneering Christian family. He was filled with the Spirit at age 4 and has since been passionate for others to experience an intimate relationship with the person of the Holy Spirit.

Julian has a seasoned prophetic ministry with a strong teaching gift and desires to see the whole Church mobilised to bring the kingdom of God onto the streets of our nations.

Julian is married to Katia and they travel and minister together extensively through the Frequentsee Trust, which serves to equip churches by establishing a revival and reformation culture.

Visit http://frequentsee.org for more information